Acclaim for
IT'S ONLY
THE JANITOR

"Through engaging stories drawn from his own remarkable career as dean, vice chancellor, and chancellor, Rod Park shares hard-won lessons—told with candor, insight, and wit—on how to succeed as an academic administrator. The stories of how he negotiated with student protesters, or restructured academic departments, or assuaged governing boards and legislators, are compelling. *It's Only the Janitor*—who cleans up the messes of others—is an enlightening and entertaining read for all new academic administrators."

— *Wallace D. Loh, Provost, University of Iowa*

"A fascinating and highly entertaining read for anyone involved in academia, administrator or not. Part autobiographical reflection by someone who has held important administrative positions at several universities, it is also a user's guide to understanding the complex workings of the university ecosystem. Writing with subtle humor and a clear style, Rod Park pulls no punches. He has been an important mentor to me and others, and this book will extend his thoughtful mentorship to a much broader audience."

— *Brent D. Mishler, Professor of Integrative Biology, Director of the University and Jepson Herbaria, UC Berkeley*

"Drawing on situations in which he was deeply involved during his long tenure at Berkeley, Rod Park has written a splendid book about administering a university. I can attest to the accuracy of his recollections, which give this book such scope, vigor, and authenticity. Moreover, he writes with clarity and zest, and his informative and entertaining presentation is full of penetrating insights."

— *Mike Heyman, Chancellor Emeritus of UC Berkeley, and former Secretary of the Smithsonian Institution*

"Rod Park was a faculty member and top administrator at the University of California at Berkeley through several tumultuous decades, which included the Free Speech Movement, the establishment of Ethnic Studies, the South African divestment struggle, the Asian American admissions crisis, and the reorganization of biology. *It's Only the Janitor* takes us through all of these events and more with wit and panache. Part history and part owner's manual, the book gives anyone interested in the world of the university lessons in its anthropology and in its leadership. As an appendix, Dr. Park includes 19th-century classicist F. M. Cornford's *Microcosmographia Academica*—a guide for 'the young academic politician.' *It's Only the Janitor* is no less, with some compelling history besides."

— *Carol Christ, President, Smith College*

IT'S ONLY
THE JANITOR

A HANDBOOK FOR NEW
ACADEMIC ADMINISTRATORS

RODERIC B. PARK

ROCKPILE
PRESS

IT'S ONLY THE JANITOR
A Handbook for New Academic Administrators
Copyright © 2010 Roderic B. Park

Rockpile Press
18450 Rockpile Road
Geyserville, CA 95441
rprockpile@gmail.com
707-272-5329

Cover design by Michael Brechner / Cypress House

Publisher's Cataloging-in-Publication Data

Park, Roderic B.
It's only the janitor : a handbook for new academic administrators / Roderic B. Park. -- 1st ed. -- Geyserville, CA : Rockpile Press, c2009.
p. ; cm.
ISBN: 978-0-9821933-8-9
Includes index.
1. College administrators--United States--Handbooks, manuals, etc. 2. College administrators--Training of--United States--Handbooks, manuals, etc. 3. Universities and colleges--United States--Administration. 4. Education, Higher--United States--Administration. I. Title. II. Title: Handbook for new academic administrators.
LB2341 .P37 2009   2009906228
378.1/110973--dc22 0912

Printed in the USA
2 4 6 8 9 7 5 3 1
First edition

# Acknowledgments

Many colleagues have contributed to my "on the job training" as I navigated the shoals, currents, and challenges of
the university. I thank all these instructors for their perception
and patience. I am forever indebted as their pupil.

Particular thanks is due my wife Catherine, herself a very accomplished administrator, for criticizing and editing my essays which
too often strayed from being a guide and wandered into inter-
esting, but irrelevant history. William Kaufmann was a constant
source of support and advice.

Cynthia Frank, Joe Shaw, Michael Brechner, and others at Cypress
House have been most generous as this manuscript made its
voyage from computer files to finished book. Their experience
and encouragement have been invaluable.

Foreword

It's Only the Janitor is a rare visit into the motivations, ambitions, and fears of the professorial mind as it influences the modern research university. This book continues insights that were initiated 100 years ago by Francis Macdonald Cornford in *Microcosmographia Academica, Being A Guide for The Young Academic Politician* (Bowes and Bowes, Cambridge, 1908). Though Cornford's little book is now out of print, it is in many ways a parent of *It's Only the Janitor* and is included in full as an appendix. While *Microcosmographia Academica* provides an accurate account of faculty attitudes during the Edwardian era, the university today is a very different institution than it was some 100 years ago. To the present-day reader, Cornford's view of the university will appear limited. Of the five parades of university marchers covered in *It's Only the Janitor*, Cornford addresses just one, the faculty member. He never mentions the word "student," though he often refers to lectures, which implies their presence. He mentions women only once (as acting by "mere instinctive intuition") and minorities not at all.

Our modern universities now enroll a vastly larger portion of society, and perform greatly increased research and public service functions while remaining the gateway to many professions. This increased societal role has been accompanied by a large increase in state and federal financial support and regulation, which in turn require that the university exhibit greater accountability for its actions from access to equal opportunity hiring to defense of the curriculum and to its role in controversial research. *It's Only the Janitor* includes these many new complexities in university life, all of which were unsuspected in Cornford's world 100 years ago.

— Richard Atkinson, former director of the National Science Foundation and President Emeritus of the University of California

IT'S ONLY
THE JANITOR

 # Contents

Introduction

So, you have been asked to take an administrative post in academia! Why should this opportunity interest you in the slightest? Assuming you are a tenured member of the faculty, you have an assured salary, time to pursue your research, office space, a paid telephone, and staff support. Who could want anything more? Administrative duties will only distract you from the major reasons you chose a faculty research career in the first place. While "pulling the levers of power" may intrigue some professors, they will soon find that the checks and balances of power in the university vastly exceed those outlined in our federal constitution. Academic administrative jobs are filled with tension and usually a lack of respect from one's former colleagues. "My friends still wave, but they don't use all their fingers" is a common observation by new faculty administrators. So, how did I become interested in administrative challenges? In retrospect, I became intrigued because effective academic administration is so challenging and yet so important to successful growth of an institution I admire—the university. How I discovered this interest is covered in chapter 1, "We are all born innocent," where an initial political defeat impelled me to start unraveling the pathways of administration.

Chapter 1

 # We Are All Born Innocent

*The number of rogues is about equal to
the number of men who act honestly;
and it is very small.*

— F. M. Cornford, *Microcosmographia Academica*

How did I, as a young faculty member who was selected for academic and not management ability, become identified for administration? Initially, I failed to follow some sound advice given by one of my older colleagues. After my first year as an assistant professor, Johannes Proskauer, a bryologist, said:

> I understand your teaching and research are progressing well. Now watch out. Soon *they* are going to ask you to start assuming administrative duties. It is important for the progress of your research that *they* leave you alone, but it is also important that you do not demonstrate incompetence. My advice is that you always do a good job on your assignment, but always hand it in late. This strategy will maintain your reputation for intelligence, but will demonstrate that you are a hopeless administrator, and *they* will stop calling on you!

In retrospect, my mistake was that I handed too many assignments in on time. And then *they* started asking me to do things.

3

My First Exposure to that Outer World: *The Muscatine Committee*

As I labored at my research and teaching as well as some departmental committee assignments, my life remained oriented around my department, the Botany Department in Berkeley's Life Sciences Building. It was not until I gained tenure, during the 1960s student movement at Berkeley, that *they* asked me to participate in broader spheres of university and faculty administration. This first exposure to industrial-strength university politics occurred at Berkeley in 1966, shortly after commencement of the Free Speech Movement (FSM) in fall 1964. The University of California's administrative structures, both at the campus and presidential level, were by temperament and process unable to deal effectively with these new challenges to traditional authority. Recognition of this failing led eventually to the replacement of Berkeley Chancellor Edward Strong by the University of California Regents in 1965, and in 1966, at the first meeting attended by newly elected Governor of California and ex officio Regent Ronald Reagan, to the firing of University President Clark Kerr. For years after, Kerr would wistfully reminisce that he left the University of California the same way that he had entered thirty years earlier, "Fired with enthusiasm."

On March 1, 1965, Acting Chancellor Martin Meyerson, who had replaced Chancellor Strong, challenged the Berkeley Academic Senate on the subject of "a pluralistic approach to education." He proposed that a new "commission on the state of education at Berkeley... bringing together and clarifying the many ideas being suggested on the campus could then develop for our consideration specific proposals for the revitalization of our educational aims and practice." The Emergency Executive Committee of the Berkeley Division of the Academic Senate presented a resolution to the full senate on March 8, 1965, which called for a Select Committee on Education at Berkeley for the following purposes:

4

- 1) To find the ways in which the traditions of humane learning and scientific inquiry can best be advanced under the challenging conditions of size and scale that confront our university community, and

- 2) To examine the various changes in educational programs currently under consideration in the several schools and colleges; to seek by appropriate means to communicate information concerning these programs to the wider campus community; and to consider the implications of these programs in the light of (1) above.

In the best tradition of any entrenched bureaucracy, the Berkeley Academic Senate created a special committee to review our educational practices for both undergraduate and graduate students in response to student unrest, and to propose changes if and where appropriate. I naively voted for this sensible proposal, confident that the task would fall on more experienced shoulders than those of a young associate professor. I left the meeting with the sense of virtue reserved for individuals who will take little or no responsibility for the action just approved. I was wrong! *They* asked me, several other Young Turks, and a few senior faculty members to serve on the new Select Committee on Education at Berkeley under the chairmanship of the noted Chaucer scholar Charles Muscatine. In a naively flattered frame of mind I said yes. We held our first meeting in mid-April 1965. One year later, on March 26, 1966, our report, including an extensive and critical minority report, was before the Academic Senate for action.

Our select committee consisted of nine Caucasian male (no female) professors who, in a racial sense at least, reflected the leadership of the student radicals as well as the administration at the time. No students served as members of the committee, although the committee had the potential for great impact on their lives. We were still living in the era of decision making by three carbon copies, and were only beginning to accommodate to the Xerox machine and how it would broaden the process of decision making in institutions.

The working year of this committee was my first field experience in faculty politics as well as my first exposure to deeply held differences about the nature of man among different academic disciplines. I stood in awe of the certainty of my older colleagues on the complex issues facing education. Only later did I realize that the problems we were working on were not new; they were merely variations on the issues universities had faced for years. What is the best way to teach undergraduates? Should we focus more on facts or on problems and ability to solve them? How do we integrate scientific inquiry into more humanistic or philosophical questions such as "Who am I? What should I know? What should I do?" and what is the role of the university in student life outside the classroom? How do we adapt to a changing student body in a way that is responsible to our scholarly commitment? Is it possible for a large and traditional institution to institutionalize experiments and change, or will change always remain so threatening to professorial ego, not to mention professorial material amenities, that change, on a time scale shorter than fifty years, is literally impossible?

Any committee is no more or no less than the beliefs, experience, and capacities of those who compose it. We were no exception. Our nine members included three humanists, two social scientists, two engineers, and two basic scientists.

Richard Herr, a professor of Spanish history, and one of the Young Turks of the mid-'60s, represented student interests and the foreign languages. It is ironic to remember that sixty years ago we were all taught that the importance of learning a foreign language was to learn about another culture, such as that of France or Germany. The thought that we would learn about truly foreign cultures such as those of the Far East or even those of our own multicultural cities never crossed our minds. There was a distinct, but unstated, definition of "culture" as meaning a form of "high culture," with others, particularly of a "primitive" sort, left to the anthropologists and associated social scientists.

Professor of psychology David Krech represented a senior, self-confident, and unreconstructed liberal wing of the faculty. He studied, among other things, the chemical basis of learning in animals, a series of studies that continue at Berkeley to the present time. Small of stature, but dominant in demeanor, impeccably dressed, and sporting a neatly trimmed Leninist beard, Krech communicated in stentorian tones that rang out even more loudly when he was challenged. He proudly taught the large freshman psychology class, and once bragged to our leader, Charles Muscatine, "Chuck, every time I give a Psychology 1 lecture it's as though I am addressing an audience of two hundred million people on CBS." Professor Muscatine responded without hesitation, "David, every time I lecture to my graduate class on Chaucer it's as though I am addressing an audience of two thousand on the BBC."

Professor of sociology Leo Lowenthal was a scholar of European intellectual history who was equally at home with historians or philosophers. As a refugee from Germany, he was better able to see Berkeley from afar than those of us who had been immersed in it, and he provided a voice of experience that the rest of us, forty years ago, had no claim to.

I, an associate professor of botany, was probably selected because of my role in reorganizing the teaching of lower-division biology at Berkeley. I had not, like some members of the committee, played an active role in the FSM and events that followed, but I was recognized to be of pragmatic mind with some capacity for leading a collegial group.

Professor George C. Pimentel was a clear-thinking physical chemist whose world was defined with the same precision as his discipline. He had been a moving force behind the improvement of high school chemistry curricula following Sputnik with the development of a new high school curriculum, and in 1969, based on infrared spectrometer measurements, predicted the Mars southern polar ice cap was water ice, not frozen carbon dioxide. If, in the parlance of the day, the humanists emphasized the Zen of education, George Pimentel emphasized the motorcycle maintenance. In his defined world, problems could be scientifically reduced to a few variables and the problem solved. That some issues can be answered only for their time was not a popular idea with George. His defined views led to continual argument with most of the rest of the committee, and eventually yielded the first profound lesson I learned in faculty politics.

Professor of mechanical engineering Samuel Schaaf had a humanistic bent. During the year our committee met, he had volunteered to participate as an instructor in a lower-division "college" under the leadership of professor of philosophy Joseph Tussman. At every meeting, Professor Schaaf would arrive with Thucydides or Herodotus under his arm. We received his lengthy views about the Peloponnesian wars, and all admired a colleague who was unafraid to move from the status of world expert in his own discipline to a new field where he integrated his knowledge into larger human questions for the benefit of undergraduates.

Professor of rhetoric Peter Dale Scott came to Berkeley by way of the Canadian Foreign Service, and thus had a predisposition toward politics. He was among those faculty members with greatest sympathy for the leaders of the student movement, and was in closest touch with them. He and Professor Herr wrote most of the material in our final report concerning students. Scott was initially a poet, but in later years his research concerned the Kennedy assassination, events surrounding the Vietnam War, and the Nixon administration. I hope it was not disillusion with the results of our committee that launched him on a new career of exposing conspiracy.

Ted Vermeulen, a professor of chemical engineering, was a

pragmatic accommodator for whom the glass was always half full and filling. When disputes flared among our membership, Ted poured the oil of his optimism on our troubled waters.

Our chairman (an acceptable term in 1965) was Charles Muscatine, a senior professor in the English department and a scholar of medieval English and French literature. A survivor of the loyalty oath controversy at Berkeley in the early 1950s, Chuck was the visionary dreamer among us. He was also articulate and tough when the occasion demanded it. He is one of the few people I have met who speaks prose and can charm and admonish with equal flair. His commitment to our task was complete.

The spectrum of our opinions on almost every issue ranged from the charitable and humanistic views of Charles Muscatine at one end to the closely defined and ordained world of George Pimentel at the other. From the amount of time students should study per week to the extent to which undergraduate students were apprentices to a great research enterprise or individuals searching for their values and identity, we always found George and Chuck at the opposite ends of the argument.

Our committee schedule during fall 1965 and spring 1966 gave us some unique opportunities to learn about each other. Of course, we learned about our colleagues' values as we discussed the educational enterprise at Berkeley, but we also learned about our deeper currents of human strength and weakness, because, during our weekend retreats in the Alumni Center at Lake Tahoe, we gambled! Typically, we would make the four-hour drive from Berkeley to Lake Tahoe late on Friday, and would spend Friday evening and all day Saturday in a small cabin just below the ski slope discussing the special topics for the weekend. Most of us looked out on the snow without any great desire to ski. The only time one of our members, Peter Scott, ventured forth to ski, he returned to the meeting on crutches. But it was not just the outdoor beauty of the Sierra Mountains that charmed our group; it was the prospect of a post-dinner visit to the gambling casinos a few miles to the east on the north shore of Lake Tahoe just beyond the Nevada border.

Our arrival at a casino was marked by the emergence of personality traits that our committee members chose not to reveal under other circumstances. George Pimentel would head straight for the craps table. To my surprise, he had an intimate knowledge of the game and its odds. As he placed his bets, the cool objective demeanor of the scientist disappeared completely. His emotional involvement was not only intense, it was total. The rest of the world disappeared. The intense gleam of his eyes, his dark hair over his forehead, and his rolled-up shirtsleeves, accompanied by a steady stream of emotional comments, did not represent the George Pimentel any of us knew. For me his actions conjured up a scene of Portuguese sailors gambling in the forepeak of the *Pinta* or *Santa Maria*. The emotional side of George was revealed because he was not responding to us, and without us there he exposed his inner self.

Leo Lowenthal, who would not think of rubbing elbows with the déclassé denizens of the craps table, went to the roulette wheel. Perhaps his exposure to European aristocracy made roulette a more acceptable pastime than slot machines or craps. Casually throwing chips on the table for long shots, he always lost rapidly, and within thirty minutes was looking for a ride back to the lodge.

Sam Schaaf also played roulette, but with an entirely different, non-flamboyant style. While Leo Lowenthal was placing chips on the board with enthusiastic abandon, Schaaf remained quietly in the background with a small stack of chips that he bet sparingly and always on the most even odds, either black and red or odd and even. By the time we left the casino, he was usually ahead by $50 or so, whereas the rest of our group was fortunate to be even. Naturally, I was curious about his low-key and successful approach, so I joined the table where he was playing. Sam would never bet unless he was playing with the house against a large better. A high roller would place $100 on red, and Sam would play $2 on black. He usually won. The same practice held on odd and even. If there were no significant bets on these squares, Sam would not play. When I asked him, "Doesn't your strategy assume that the house is controlling the roulette wheel?" he responded, "No, I have just noticed that the house always seems to win."

The remainder of us played lesser games and slot machines, which had the advantage that, by the time we returned to the alumni center, we each had $5 or so in change for a friendly poker game. Our three poker games during that year all followed the same pattern. Charles Muscatine, David Krech, and Leo Lowenthal were generally the first to leave the game, followed shortly by Dick Herr and Peter Scott. Next to go was Ted Vermeulen, which left the chemist George Pimentel, the engineer Sam Schaaf, and me, the botanist Rod Park. After a few hands, George, whose frowns and smiles telegraphed his hand, would be out of the game, leaving Sam and me. We would then set a time limit, and Sam and I could never conclude with an ultimate winner. We could not read each other's hands. Only later did I realize that we were the only two members of the committee who were concerned just about the game and not the money.

Through our gambling, we all learned how to read each other better. I could often read the bluffs of my colleagues as well as their hidden pain on losing, and our deliberations became more effective. I suggest that this exercise, never recommended in any management workshop that I have attended, is a remarkably effective introduction to the debating strategies of your colleagues.

The result of our yearlong effort was a report of almost 200 pages. It covered Berkeley students, improvement of teaching, freshman admissions, advising, grading, a board of educational development, new programs, graduate education, and the training and duties of teaching assistants. Through all the discussions, the polarization between George Pimentel and the rest of the committee remained. George more and more felt he was the Horatio of our committee, and it was his role to protect the quality of graduate education at Berkeley against the more suspect agendas of other committee members. Our discussion of each draft topic would be approaching agreement when George would say, "Charles, I really can't go along with this sentence (or this recommendation) without the following changes." Of course, George's changes invariably argued for less change, and exuded greater institutional satisfaction with the status quo.

I observed that our spirit of collegiality abetted this process, and the report that came to the committee for final approval showed the effects of George's persistence. I, along with the committee, believed George had accomplished his goal and was satisfied.

At our final meeting for report approval, George made a surprise announcement, to the naive young professors like me at least. "Charles," he said, "I was up all night worrying about this report. I have decided I cannot go along with it, and ask that you give me three days to write a minority report for inclusion with that of the majority." We had bent the majority report a considerable distance from its initial thrust to accommodate Professor Pimentel, and he was writing a minority report anyway! Three days later my dismay increased when George arrived with a forty-page, single-spaced, typewritten alternative report with detailed recommendations and arguments for consideration by the Academic Senate. What George had to say was carefully and fully argued. I could only conclude that I had spent three months compromising with a man who was each night writing a minority report and thus taking two bites of the apple. George taught me a lesson I have never forgotten. A slightly cynical version is: **age and treachery will always take the field against mere youth and skill.**

My naiveté intrigued me. Why had this happened, and what

could I learn about getting things done in the university that would put me on the sending end and not on the receiving end of such political gambits? How could I become an effective agent for needed change? By asking these questions, I took my first steps down a road that would forever differentiate me from my colleagues. I would, by degrees, leave the faculty fraternity and join the "administration," a suspect but necessary institution in the academy. I would find out what that outer world beyond my academic department was like, and how to become an effective agent of desired change.

To succeed as "an agent of desired change" the young faculty member must learn some new skills, usually not part of the Ph.D. curriculum. Most recent Ph.D. recipients never had a course in leadership, administration, or management. Such lack of preparation, while by no means a disqualifying omission, is a disadvantage. The ego of a faculty member is often large enough to perceive leadership and management as lesser skills than academic creativity, and to suppose that they are easily mastered. In fact, many faculty members have become excellent administrators through "on the job training," but most have not. Ask any faculty member in a college with rotating departmental chairs and you will soon become aware that administrative unevenness in departmental leadership is the rule and not the exception. Similarly, deans recruited from within the faculty, unless we are talking about a large institution, are often uneven in administrative performance.

But faculty members are by their very nature "quick learners," and when given a few basic principles underlying academic administration are more likely to succeed. This small volume attempts such a tutorial. But before recounting actual administrative case studies, we cover the landscape of constituencies you are about to traverse, namely the deepest beliefs and fears of faculty members, students, alumni, temporary faculty, staff, and governing boards. While technology and economic circumstances change rapidly, the fundamental behaviors of these university actors do not! How professors, students, alumni, staff, trustees, and local officials interact is much the same today as it was one hundred or more years ago.

For those who doubt the persistent roles university actors play on academia's stage, read F. M. Cornford's *Microcosmographia Academica*. First published in 1908 by Bowes and Bowes, Cambridge, this short essay, reproduced as an appendix here, is available on the Internet*and is required reading for any new university administrator!

---

* Original edition of Internet copy printed in Cambridge, Mass., by Metcalf & Company LTD.

Chapter 2

The University as a Parade

Talking to the students is like talking to a parade.
— Roger Heyns, Former Berkeley Chancellor*

In the same way that herds of animals outlive the many indi-vidual creatures that compose them, universities outlive the individuals that, at any time, are their faculty members, staff, trustees, administrators, or students. If the active life of a faculty member is thirty-five years, then Harvard, established in 1636, is about ten and one half generations of faculty in age. Similarly, many nonacademic staff at the university spend their entire careers working in academia, and their duration of association with the institution often approaches that of faculty members.'

The lifetime of university administrators is much shorter than that of faculty members, and has become still shorter since the civil rights movement and the student movement of the 1960s. Since WW II, the balance of national values has moved away from respect for institutions, toward increased respect for individuals and individual differences. This change has made a university president with more than seven to eight years' ten-ure an endangered species. Increased numbers of organized

---

* Often said in speeches to UC Berkeley faculty members.

15

constituencies competing for certification by the university (a circumstance described by Arthur M. Schlesinger Jr. in *The Disuniting of America* as *pluribus* overbalancing *unum)** as well as scarce resources have taken their toll on the longevity of university administrations at most institutions.

Trustees generally serve for ten to twenty years, and thus, properly, have terms slightly longer than the president they are responsible for hiring or replacing.

---

* Arthur M. Schlesinger Jr., *The Disuniting of America,* Whittle Direct Books, 1991, p. 80.

The life of the student within the institution is much shorter. If the attendance of graduate and undergraduate students at the university averages five years, Harvard has existed for seventy-four generations of students, compared with only ten for faculty. Students, like it or not, become alumni who go on a march of their own, often reflecting the university as they knew it when they were undergraduates.

The university, then, can be seen as five parades all marching at different rates through the institution. The slowest marchers are the faculty and the staff. The view that those who march most slowly will know the most about the institution and should therefore have the most to say about its future is only partly true. Trustees march about twice as fast as the faculty, and the administration at about three times the faculty rate. The students march most rapidly of all, traversing the university in only four to five years.

As might be expected, faculty members, who have the longest span of association with the institution as well as tenure, tend to be the curators of tradition in the academy. It is true that there are some faculty members with sincerely held views in favor of change, but when it comes to a vote in the Academic Senate, these forces rarely carry the day. Though radical faculty numbers would appear to grow through new recruitment, these numbers also diminish with the increasing age of the incumbents, who often become tempered or exhausted by experience.

If the slowest marchers, the faculty, ultimately play a conservative role at the university, the students, who march most rapidly, might be thought of as the harbingers of change, particularly the student governments who have only nine months to improve and humanize their alma mater.

The administration and the trustees march at an intermediate speed, often mediating what appears to be the proper course between demands for excessive change by the students and legislatures, and faculty insistence on no change at all. Effective change that better adapts the institution to its political and financial environment without sacrificing its intellectual integrity is always in order. As stated by the art historian Robert Byron, "Misfortune comes to the complacent, brought not by some moral law, but because complacence is the parent of incompetence."[*]

Each group of marchers has its own culture and its own tribal totems and taboos. What they have in common is a belief in intellectual enlightenment, though their answers will differ when they are asked how to achieve it. Part of the difference results because most of the human issues addressed by the university have no absolute answers. A university has two sorts of problems: those it can solve, and those it can only work on. Both kinds require great effort, but the second kind requires great perseverance as well. The problems that a university can solve permanently are bounded and discrete, such as engineering and mathematics problems or the erection of a building. But the most common problems are of the second kind. They are of a human sort, and can be solved only for a limited time and for a specific group of people. Succeeding generations will demand rearguing, rethought, and new solutions. This second class of problems is perennial, and has classically constituted the subject matter for a liberal education. These problems range from the content of the curriculum, to standards of morality, to strategies for world peace and the eradication of sin, to a syllabus for the freshman composition course, and to individual answers to the questions, "What can I know?", "What should I do?", "What may I hope for?", and "What is man?" After a truly effective liberal education, the recipient will have informed positions on these subjects and many more. In addition, these students will be open

---

[*] As quoted by D. P. Moynihan, *On The Law of Nations,* Harvard University Press (1990), p. 147.

to new arguments throughout their lifetimes. Only when they become ossified in their positions about problems that have no absolute answers will they have grown old.

The problems and potentials of a university become more comprehensible if one first considers the five cultural parades of faculty, students, administrators, staff, and trustees that pass through it. Each parade embodies its own customs as well as its own strengths and weaknesses. University issues of the second kind, such as undergraduate curriculum, free speech, access, leadership, and case studies of effective and ineffective attempts at change within the university take on deeper meaning when we see them as related to the parades. My recollections here will have achieved their objective if they make the path, or art of the possible, within the academy clearer to those who have the youth and temerity to change and improve it. Without some foreknowledge of the tribal structures of the university, young academic politicians will usually have expended their small bank accounts of administrative credibility before their plans are even off the drawing board (or computer screen). I am reminded of a statement by a new dean at Berkeley who was recruited from another university. Several days after he arrived, I asked him how he was getting along. He replied: "I arrived in my office and greeted the staff. My desk had upon it the levers of power and only a small list of tasks left by my predecessor. I spoke with the student and faculty leadership, and by the second afternoon decided to start pulling some levers. It wasn't until a day later I found that the levers were not connected to anything!"

May these sketches of the deepest aspirations and fears of the academy's inhabitants aid the continuing parade of young academic politicians like yourself as you strive to become effective.

Chapter 3

The Faculty: Curators of Tradition

*It is impossible to enjoy the contemplation of
truth if one is vexed and distracted by
the sense of responsibility*

— F. M Cornford

"The faculty" is a collective term, which implies that faculty members are of one mind on most issues. This assumption does great disservice to the decentralized organization of the faculty and to the diversity of opinion that exists. Except, perhaps, for salaries and the three unifying issues discussed in this chapter, the level of faculty member agreement in most institutions is about the same as that in the French Assembly. A statement attributed to Robert Gordon Sproul captured this insight when he said about the faculty, "The Academic Senate is a group of individuals who think otherwise!" The diversity of which he spoke is one of age, of education, of orientation toward intellectual and practical problems, of political outlook, and of relationship to students, citizens, legislators, and colleagues.

This diversity is further stimulated by the plain fact that many faculty members are totally removed from the political and financial forces buffeting their institutions. They do not read the campus newspaper or go to Academic Senate meetings or participate in fundraising. They never enter more than one or two of the one hundred major buildings on campus unless they attend a lecture or find it necessary to deal with the bureaucracy of the institution—for instance, in filing grades or resisting a parking ticket. For scientists, in particular, searching the Internet has made trips to the library almost unnecessary. Faculty members have also developed great skill at reducing the voluminous mail they receive to the bare minimum of required reading. They speak with their intellectual friends within and without the university, teach their classes, go occasionally to department meetings, collect data, and prepare their findings for publication. To a great extent, their sense of self-worth is established by the recognition they receive from their peers and their students. They also appreciate recognition from their institution, particularly when it is reflected in a promotion or a merit pay increase, but for many if not most faculty members, status is achieved primarily through external recognition in the form of external research reviews, award of grants, recognition by professional societies, and invitations to be major speakers at national or international meetings. Recognition doesn't always have to take the form of praise. Some faculty members (I can think of a few at Berkeley and Boulder) would rather be vilified than neglected!

Against this background of decentralized interest, the institution, through its administration, is called upon by concerned citizens, including many faculty, administrators, parents, and students, to provide a unified and coherent general education for undergraduates, a broad and fundamental training for graduate students, and useful service for the community. These missions must be built on the feudal separatism of individual faculty members and departmental interests.

Assuming that changes are sometimes necessary to improve an institution, those responsible for providing leadership in the university, whether faculty or administration, must devise strategies that have some probability of bringing about such change. But before one can make changes in a university, one must get the faculty's attention. This is not as easy as it might seem, because many faculty members possess a remarkable ability to continue minding their own business when beckoned by larger institutional responsibilities. As mentioned in chapter 14, you can lead a horse to water, but you can't make it drink. Even to lead faculty members to water, you must first make them think it is their idea.

If the faculty is by nature decentralized and faculty members self-concerned,*there are three classic dramas in academia that command immediate attention and awaken righteous unity among faculty members from their generally dormant state. The first classic drama is a real or perceived attack on the tenure system. The second drama is a similar challenge to academic freedom. The third drama is a perceived attack, generally budgetary, on one's department or intellectual home, which faculty members usually translate as institutional disregard for their chosen life commitment to a field of research.

Attacks on tenure – Tenure is an institutional policy, developed by the 1920s, which holds that a faculty member can be fired only for cause and not for unpopular teachings, research, or political views. Faculty members under a tenure system, after they have proven their ability to create and present new scholarship or performance, are assured that research and teaching in politically or morally unpopular areas is not a basis for separation from the institution so long as their scholarship is sound,

---

* "Self-concern" is a way of saying that a primary fuel necessary for the successful research university is gratification of faculty ego. The other institution that is equally ego driven is the state legislature, with which the public university interacts. There are, however, some important differences. Faculty members have tenure; legislators are constantly running for office. Faculty members do not have to pay close attention to what the public thinks; legislators do. Faculty members, for the most part, like their jobs; most politicians, particularly those with term limits, are by nature dissatisfied and are always looking toward their next post. Staff members in the university almost never become faculty members; staff members in the legislature often rise to political office.

23

other obligations to the institution are met, and their activities are legal. Under the policies of the American Association of Universities (AAU), the apprenticeship of an untenured faculty member may last for up to eight years, a period generally consisting of four two-year contracts, before final action is required to decide whether he or she gains tenure or not. During the seventh year a decision must be made for "up or out"—that is, the faculty member is promoted to tenure or his or her contract is not renewed beyond the eighth year. Actually, few non-tenured faculty members require the full eight years to gain tenure, and most cases are decided in six years or less. Nonetheless, though long periods of time are required to demonstrate scholarly competence in most fields, when compared with personnel policies of other institutions in the United States, an apprenticeship of up to eight years to gain permanent career status, while appropriate for a university, assumes the dimensions of an anachronistic medieval holdover. In contrast, clerical staff members in academic departments receive the legal equivalent of tenure at the end of their probationary period, usually just ninety days, rather than eight years.

Tenure was established, not to protect incompetent or lazy faculty members, but rather those productive scholars and teachers with politically or morally unpopular views or areas of research. Unfortunately the definition of tenure has become much broader and now implies to many citizens that tenured faculty members are immune to firing under any circumstances. To be sure, only a small percentage of tenured faculty members— some estimate, and I agree, about 3 percent—are not performing adequately. At present, the threshold of "low performance" in research and teaching sufficient to separate a faculty professor from a tenured position is so low that most institutions of higher education would be embarrassed to reduce their criteria to written form. In recent years, tenure and "security of employment" have become almost synonymous terms.

One now often hears the opinion that a tenured faculty member who has stopped doing research and whose teaching has not kept up with research advances cannot be dismissed even after performance review and warnings.*To use the 1980s term applied to defaulted bank loans, such a faculty member might be called "non-performing." What is the definition of a non-performing professor? First, it is well known that scholarly creativity for most academics varies throughout one's life with both productive and fallow periods. In highly theoretical areas such as mathematics or physics, for example, it is common for scholars to accomplish their most creative work before they are forty years old. In the humanities, where creativity is usually based on wide acquaintanceship with past scholarship, creativity often occurs later in one's academic's career. Does this mean that theoretical physicists or mathematicians should be dismissed at age fifty when their research productivity has diminished or, in some cases, dried up? General wisdom and practice says no, not if they are still continuing to teach effectively, guide graduate research, and aid in the administration of their institution. Once a faculty member has gained tenure, there are very few cases when that protection is questioned. At institutions such as Berkeley, tenure questions never involve established and productive faculty citizens. They involve generally those few faculty members who have become less productive researchers and less effective teachers and whose performance sometimes crosses the line of negligence. More often than not, their diminishing performance is related to ill health, alcoholism, or personal tragedy in their

---

* It is a matter of public record that in 1991 a tenured member of the UC Berkeley faculty was dismissed after being charged with sexual harassment and going through an extensive due process procedure. The adjudication process took nearly three years. In 2006 a UC Boulder academic committee confirmed that a professor was guilty of academic misconduct, including plagiarism. In July 2007, by an 8 to 1 vote, the University of Colorado Board of Regents fired him.

private lives. A sign of a capable administration is its ability to resolve such touchy situations either through improved performance or by a negotiated separation from the university without a hearing before the faculty Committee on Privilege and Tenure, which assumes the dimensions of a "competency" trial.

Tenure is more a concern of the apprentices, the assistant professors who have not yet achieved it, than of the tenured faculty. As mentioned above, assistant professors, under AAU and university policy, must qualify for tenure within eight years of full employment or leave the university. During their apprenticeship, they are expected to develop their teaching programs and to produce research that is nationally recognized in their fields. These apprentice faculty are extensively reviewed many times during their eight years with respect to their teaching, research, and public service, and tenure is never a question in the strongest and weakest cases. Only in marginal cases is the question raised: "Was I denied tenure for improper discrimination because of my sex, race, religion, or geographic origin?"

The word "discrimination" has, in the past forty years, come to have a negative context in American English, because it is generally used as shorthand for "illegal discrimination." Every time we scan a restaurant menu, we discriminate among the offerings, but we are discriminating legally. The tenure decision itself discriminates between the most competent and other, lesser, competitors who are "deselected." It is vital that illegal discrimination not enter the process.

Attacks on Academic freedom – Attacks upon academic freedom that can be nobly resisted are rare. We seldom get a clear-cut case in which, for example, a trustee writes a letter commanding a professor to change the political content of a course or to sign a loyalty oath (this happened at the University of California in 1952) if the faculty member is to continue in the employ of the institution. The most publicized such case at Berkeley within the last forty years occurred in fall 1968, when

the best-selling author of *Soul on Ice*, Black Panther Information Minister and Peace and Freedom Party candidate—albeit
felon on parole—Eldridge Cleaver was invited to give ten lectures in an experimental course in the Sociology Department
(see p. 86). The University of California Regents were violently
opposed. In retaliation they almost removed responsibility for
approval of courses from the faculty, a responsibility they had
been delegated in 1920. This case was defended by the administration in the face of passionate and unfavorable public opinion.

Challenges to academic freedom are seldom so dramatic.
They are more often cast in the gray zone between the prerogatives of an individual faculty member and the perceived integrity of the institution. For example, should a professor of physics
be allowed to teach for credit a social science course on the
politics of arms control? If insufficient departmental research
space causes denial of faculty grant applications and thus denial
of rapid academic promotion, is this a denial of academic freedom? Is interruption of a public lecture by hecklers a denial of
academic freedom, and if so, what level of heckling is to be tolerated? Disruption of speakers and the corresponding attack on
academic freedom became an all-too-common event at Berkeley in the early to mid-1980s. Disruption was always justified on
the grounds that the moral imperative of the issue was so great
that it justified suspending the rules.*

---

* One of the great ironies in the city of Berkeley during the 1970s and 1980s
has been its public image of extreme tolerance, whereas, in fact, speech free
of heckling and interruption was often allowed only to speakers confirming
the beliefs of the political left. Politically correct (PC) radical groups appeared
to believe that no PC person should have to listen to opinions that he did not
like, and that he should instead censor such utterances. As administrators,
those of us introducing conservative lecturers on the Berkeley campus in the
1980s came with a prepared statement in our pockets. Mine read as follows:
  "Ladies and Gentlemen:
  "In order to insure our rights of peaceful assembly and of free speech, the
  ushers and police are instructed to enforce the laws created to protect
  those rights. The ushers will ask those who disrupt this ceremony to cease

Academic freedom issues are another example of the large set of problems that do not have exact or final solutions. They are solved in the context of a specific time and circumstance through a process that has credibility with the faculty, the students, and their external publics, including the administration. Again, these issues are not solved in the manner of an engineering problem; they are problems that we must continue to work on, problems that every generation of faculty and administration must review and recertify.

Attacks on departmental budgets – Departments, an invention of universities stemming back to 1825, are a mechanism for dealing with the explosion of knowledge in the eighteenth and nineteenth centuries. Though the first academic department was founded by Harvard in 1825, departments were not common until President Charles William Eliot introduced departments to Harvard in the 1860s. This development followed the foundation of many professional academic societies during the previous twenty years.

Departments became an association of scholars who provide specialized research training for doctoral students and generate new knowledge in specific fields. The departmental structure has produced enormous benefits in research, but at the same time has isolated many faculty members from a broader intellectual acquaintance with their university. A major difficulty with presentation of a coherent program to today's undergraduates is that professors, while conversant with their own specialized areas, are for the most part much less informed about the

---

their disruption. If they continue, the ushers will ask them to leave the auditorium. If they refuse to do so, the police will take them out.

"We have no hesitancy in doing this because we must protect freedom of speech, and because the campus offers many opportunities for all to make their opinions known. Those opportunities do not extend to suppressing the free speech of others by disruption.

"I am sure you understand this and support it."

larger educational challenges facing the university. Even if they become informed, they are often uncomfortable about teaching material belonging to other academic departments because they would no longer be "world experts," and therefore would be subject to criticism from their more specialized colleagues.

Most faculty members have never seen a ledger sheet for their department, and if they did, many would find it irrelevant. From the vantage point of a faculty member, the issues are: Can I get my material typed when I want it? Is the book I need in the library, and can someone get it for me? Are my graduate students supported through teaching, research, or fellowship positions? Is my telephone bill paid? Do I have a parking space? Will the administration replace someone in the academic field of my colleague who is retiring next year? Why is the administration allowing department X to hire an expert in my field? (This person might attract students and thus budgetary support from my department.)

The relationship of these immediate concerns to larger budgetary issues is generally reduced to "the dean just doesn't understand our problems or our importance; once we explain it, he/she will restore our budget!" In the same way that one-issue groups wish to be certified by the university, so do faculty members. This departmental certification generally falls into two categories, faculty positions* and space. Increase in either, or preferably both, of these categories means that one is part of an intellectual enterprise that is perceived by campus

---

* Faculty positions are generally referred to as FTE or Full Time Equivalents. A full-time faculty member would occupy 1.0 FTE, whereas a half-time faculty member occupies 0.5 FTE. In most state universities, the number of funded faculty FTEs is calculated from the number of student credit hours (SCH) generated through course work. By state standards, one student is defined as 15 units of course work generated for each of two semesters during the year, or a total of $2 \times 15 = 30$ SCH. The student/faculty ratio at the University of California is about 20/1. This means that 1.0 FTE faculty members must generate on average 30×20 or 600 SCH per year to justify their positions.

decision makers as important. Correspondingly, a decrease in either category is initially dismissed as a mistake on the part of an administration that just doesn't understand. If a subsequent appeal is denied, righteous outrage is soon replaced by demoralization and despair, unless a very clear case has been built by the administration. Of these two resources, faculty positions and space, one is temporary. Faculty members eventually leave the institution. They take other positions, retire, or die. Space, on the other hand, is relatively permanent. Though faculty members leave, the space they occupied remains. If "the territorial imperative" is a defining motivation for all primates, it is doubly so for faculties. The only way space for a declining department can be taken away and given to an expanding program is first by fiat—which is almost certain to cause a cry of denial of academic freedom—or second, by academic reorganization. It is almost impossible to eliminate any academic administrative structure within the university outright. The uproar from the alumni, legislature, and students would be deafening. It is reorganization with incentives by which the object is attained.

What people outside the university often fail to recognize is that faculty members usually do not see themselves as part of a team of the kind that one might find in the outside world. In industry, one generally has a job description that defines one's role with specific duties that make up part of an overall team effort. Tenure-track faculty members, on the other hand, all have the same job description (teaching, research, and public service) and are part of a team only in that they were generally hired to work in some recognized area of their departmental discipline. Remaining in this area is largely up to the faculty member, who may, under the assurances of academic freedom, but usually with skepticism from colleagues, move from chemistry to biochemistry or from theoretical particle physics to astrophysics, for example. In this sense, faculty members compete with each other for institutional recognition in the form not only of salary but also of space. For the most part, faculty members lead fairly independent academic lives, and circle their wagons for common defense only when tenure, academic freedom, or budget are threatened. Many faculty members, particularly in the sciences, engineering, and business administration, have forgone larger financial rewards offered by the private sector in order to pursue their own ideas in their own ways and at their own pace. Institutional interference with their individual journeys is not appreciated. It is hard to argue with their position.

One final issue also unifies faculty members. Though it seems trivial to those who have not endured the debates it engenders, it is a passionate subject based on a deep sense of primate territoriality—parking! Faculty members work odd hours, coming and going during the day and the night, and they cherish the belief that the university should supply convenient parking for each faculty member as a free benefit. The State of California has deemed otherwise, and parking facilities must be funded from the revenues generated by the people who park in them. The Academic Senate at UC Berkeley became exercised enough on this contentious issue to appoint a Committee on Parking to represent faculty views to the administration. Some of the finest legal minds from Boalt Hall willingly sit on this committee to argue and negotiate with the administration over parking rates and parking availability.

Chapter 4

The Students – Harbingers of Change

*Young people are like young trees. You have
to prune them up once in a while, but for
the most part you just let them grow!*
— W. M. Laetsch

Without students there would be no university. True, there
is a college at the University of Oxford, England—All
Souls College—that has no students, but it is hard to imagine
that it could be an attractive place without the rest of the Oxford
colleges surrounding it. Without the constant rebellious spirit
of youth as applied to intellectual matters, the fellows of such
a college would always be in danger of becoming complacent.
Recall the wisdom of Robert Byron (p.17) that "complacence is
the parent of incompetence."

Students are to a college as children are to a family. They are
a joy, a delight to observe as they grow to intellectual and physical maturity, and at times they are also the subjects of despair
and disappointment. Being a professor or academic administrator is like having an endless number of offspring. As we grow
older, each year brings to the university a new group of young
people who remain the same age. It is soon apparent that these
rows of student marchers do not change; year after year, each
row comes with about the same level of intellectual and social
maturity. It is a renewal to watch the marchers evolve, not only

in their academic skills and creativity, but also in their maturation with respect to the larger questions in our society, which only they can answer for themselves.

In the spring of 1986, I came to know an adversary of the administration in the person of a talented undergraduate woman who was later to attend Oxford University as a Marshall Scholar. She had not been much involved in the larger world of university politics until she became deeply committed to the South African divestment issue and spent much of the 1986 spring semester sleeping on the Sproul Hall steps as part of a "live- in" to protest University of California investment policies. I occasionally took her to lunch at The Faculty Club and listened to her anger directed at me and the rest of the administration for our "insensitivity and cowardice" and for our reluctance to go to the mat with the regents over their color-blind investment policies. I responded to her outbursts, not with hostility, but with questions, because she had great ability that I hoped to protect from her consuming anger. I tried to explain that UC, Berkeley, despite its imperfections, listened to student protesters as I was listening to her and that the institution was not the oppressor she imagined. Several months later I received a note from Oxford. She said in part, "This is a real 'Dorothy from Kansas I want to go home letter. This place is suffering from years of financial and intellectual neglect. Thank you for believing in me." We were both redeemed. This was the greatest reward I could receive from one of my students.

Again, marchers present two sorts of problems: those we can solve, and those we can only work on. Most problems are of the second kind. Student marchers are particularly concerned about the rules of the university with respect to political advocacy, free speech, and discipline, or the assignment of grades and the appeals process. They eventually discover that the faculty is in charge, and that their education in this sense is not a democratic process. To some new students, university rules and practices that limit student desires for change are seen as unwarranted restrictions. Often students will assume that complex problems must have simple answers, and only the selfish motives of adults prevent their solutions from being implemented. Their suspicions might be partly true, but closer analysis often indicates that the problem is one that succeeding generations will engage, perhaps with no possibility of a final solution. Most difficult and common problems of the second kind are solved only for a limited time, by and for the university marchers who at that point are traversing the institution. Succeeding generations will demand rearguing, rethought, and new approaches. Our belief in liberal education is that the best education is not prescriptive, but lets students develop their own answers to questions that have no exact answers. Our questioning environment leads to discomfort for many who do not believe in questioning dearly held values.

To any Berkeley administrator the most familiar forum for discussing student activism is during question-and-answer sessions at alumni and community functions. The question is politely stated, "When are you going to teach those students how to behave?" or less politely "When is your gutless administration going to stand up to that radical rabble and set a proper moral tone for the university?" These questions emerge from people who are deeply offended by the behavior of some students, and often are even more deeply offended by the questions raised, which may challenge the most cherished values of large segments of our society.

The irony of this situation is that no matter how much knowledge and experience our society accumulates, every child is born naive. In fact, there is no evidence that a newborn today is any more sophisticated about the world, and particularly those problems of the second type, than the newborn human brought into the world by a hunting and gathering group of 20,000 years ago. This became evident to me as, each fall, I would meet with the new student government at Berkeley to discuss the "issues" and to develop a process for addressing them. On occasion, I was tempted to say, "But we went through all that last year." I did not say it, because I soon realized that if institutions have short memories, student government has almost none at all. I was, in fact, teaching a class on government and institutions. It was much like teaching freshman chemistry or English composition. It did no good to say, "I taught that last year" any more than to say, "I taught these students calculus last year, why are they raising the same questions again?" Roger Heyns was right when he said, "talking to the students is like talking to a parade." As soon as the workings of the institution are explained to one group of students, another group comes along, and we start the discussion all over again. This realization can sustain administrators when they recall, "But we went through all that last year!"

Student Protest

How do youth learn and beyond this become wise about problems with no absolute solutions? Parents who have dealt with a two-year-old or a teenager know that no matter how carefully they explain lessons of the past, their beliefs and assumptions will always be tested. In fact, much of undergraduate education, whether in the sciences or in courses emphasizing human values, stresses the need for students to determine for themselves the validity of what they read or hear. Students are expected to mature and become strong through mental exercise, not to become fat from unquestioned nurture. A developed intellect must be skeptical about the sales pitches that inundate us daily from corrupt promoters who promise wealth, beauty, or popularity—just send your money—and from political saviors on the right and left who propose simple solutions to complex problems and who also solicit your resources as you join their "ministries." We teach, or should teach, our students to receive such sloganeering with the question "Exactly what is the evidence for that statement?" Our democracy is most strengthened by those who have questioned and subsequently reaffirmed the faith of their elders, arriving at their own relationships to the society around them. Political activism is, for many intellectually vigorous students, a necessary step toward reaffirmed faith in our political system.

The problem for a university administration is how to keep activism from repressing the rights of others and to remain within the bounds of law. This is a difficult and narrow path. The governor, the legislators, alumni, parents, local citizens, and donors both corporate and private all have a stake in the external perceptions of student activism. The governor, because he is an ex officio member of the Board of Regents of the University, is seen by the public as bearing a direct responsibility for university activities and welfare; the legislators have a stake because their constituents are the parents of most of the students and because Ronald Reagan showed them in 1966 that running against disorder at the university is a useful election vehicle; the alumni have a stake because they often view any trouble at the university as diminishing the value of their degrees as they recall a "golden age" when they attended CAL; local citizens have a stake because the university is a large and imposing bureaucracy on their doorstep, and in the view of some is perennially insensitive and out of control; donors have a stake because a gift is much like an investment, and who is going to invest in an institution that does not have control of itself?

The path of the administration is further complicated by the fact that since the mid-1960s, campuses like Berkeley have become both national and international media theater. Political activity and espousing of social causes at UC Berkeley are as likely, or more likely, to gain media attention as on any other national campus. The most effective strategy for an activist group desiring such attention is to move into the gray zone of acceptable conduct and precipitate a conflict with police in front of television cameras. Whereas commercial advertisers pay hundreds of thousands of dollars for a few one-minute spots on national television, the effective activist can get equivalent exposure for almost nothing.

When Protest Subverts the Educational Process

Universities are, or should be, bastions of free speech and political expression. At the same time, they must also accomplish their educational missions of teaching, research, and public service. When these values come into conflict, the mettle of the administration is most tested. Time, place, and manner rules*define where and when rallies may occur and whether sound amplification may be used. These regulations are designed to assure that rallies and marches do not interfere with the education of students wanting to attend class, or with the right of faculty members to teach them. But protesters know that the best way to recruit others to their cause is to foment a confrontation between the students and the administration by treading the gray zones surrounding acceptable conduct. Remember that students are selected for admission to the university because of their intelligence, creativity, and unique experiences. If student protests are an inevitable part of a liberal education, then an administration can anticipate new and unexpected forms of protest that fall into the gray zone of behavior, somewhere between acceptable and actionable.

---

* During the FSM controversy in 1964, the Academic Senate called upon the campus to develop time, place, and manner rules that would be consistent with the educational functions of the campus. These rules designate free speech areas, time, and amount of amplification, reservations for use, qualifications of users, and other matters now covered in more than 300 regulations from the Office of Student Affairs.

Testing the Gray Zones

During the third world strike of 1969, rallies in Sproul Plaza, which were to terminate at 1:00 p.m., were continued as noisy marches through campus buildings by several hundred protesters. They moved rapidly, often armed with spray paint for defacing corridors. I recall following such marches through the Life Sciences building with paper towels and a bottle of acetone to remove the paint before it dried. Campus police could not keep up in sufficient numbers to halt the practice.

Another tactic was to go to the library and "reshelve the books." A few hundred students in the library for a few days could move books six or ten feet away from their catalogued space, rendering a chief resource of the university almost useless. Reshelving was and remains almost impossible to control. Not only are librarians unaccustomed to patrolling their stacks for "reshelvers" and apprehending them, such actions provided Teflon defenses for a student conduct hearing: "I was just browsing in the stacks." Reshelving, in addition to making the library fairly useless, forced the university to pay large sums for returning volumes to their assigned places.

An additional gray zone tactic emerged at Berkeley during the apartheid protests of 1986, in which my student friend, the Marshall Scholar, participated. Activists decided to convert the "sit-in" to a "live-in" on a visible part of the university that is not ordinarily subject to daily closure. Their tactic was day-round occupation of the steps of Sproul Hall, which faces the major plaza of the campus and was the birth site of the FSM in fall 1964. Because there is no regular time at which the university closes the steps, it was hard to argue legally that public occupancy could not occur at all hours. Also, though overnight lodging is not permitted on university grounds, it could be argued that some occupants were awake at all times, and how did this differ from a boring class? The occupation of the steps continued for many weeks, until by mutual agreement the action ceased just before graduation week.

Recent years have seen a formalization of one protest scenario that has all the elements of a pageant. The action, usually a sit-in, is sustained beyond the closing time of the building. The police announce that any protester remaining in the building will be subject to arrest. Some protesters leave, and others, usually with a prior agreement with the police, remain to be cited. The protesters who choose not to be cited remain outside to cheer those who have been cited and released as they emerge from the building, often with an arm raised in the Black Power salute.

An important principle has emerged from protesters' actions that cross the gray zone into acts of civil disobedience. If the protesters are arrested and charges pressed, there is always a request for clemency based on the political and ethical morality of the act for which the arrests were made. The argument against clemency is simple and realistic. What gives an act of civil disobedience its significance is the fact that the protesters believe so strongly in what they perceive as an injustice that they are willing to accept the legal consequences of their act. For an administration to grant amnesty in such circumstances is to remove the moral significance of the act itself.

One action of student protester strikes at the core of free speech and at the conduct of intellectual inquiry: the denial of free speech to others. Can conservative speakers give their own views in a campus classroom setting without being shouted down? How does the administration maintain control of the lecture so that an opposing point of view may be heard?

Political Correctness and Free Speech

Education is the ability to listen to almost anything without losing your temper or your self confidence.
— Robert Frost, US Poet (1874–1963)

It is ironic that the extension of free speech to political advocacy on the Berkeley campus, which was secured by the student movement in 1964, would soon become subverted by later marchers in that same parade. The new campus policy allowed political advocacy on campus in designated free speech areas. This was, in theory, a logical appendage to academic freedom for faculty, which already existed within the framework of course content and the classroom. Though the leader of the FSM, Mario Savio, had achieved his goal and disbanded his followers, those who had tasted the excitement of confrontation with authority decided to further test the limits of free speech. In early 1965 they established what became known as "the filthy speech movement." A fundamental first amendment principle was rapidly reduced to its lowest common denominator.

But subversion of free speech on the Berkeley campus was to develop most strongly during the 1970s and 1980s in parallel with the radicalization of the city of Berkeley itself. As the radical left came to power in Berkeley politics, that sense of power was shared by many politically motivated students. These students had been instrumental in bringing the Berkeley Citizen Action (BCA) party to office in city government and shared much of its vision. But power, as it often does, began to corrupt, largely because the "vision" was monolithic and had no room for those with opposing views.

The corruption was fueled initially by legitimate issues. There was moral outrage against the Vietnam War and the draft, which wound down in the early 1970s. This anger was sustained by United States involvement in Central America,

41

and a perceived lack of institutional and governmental concern with the apartheid policy of South Africa. The seeming intransigence of government on these issues produced a frustration that fueled the drive toward a radical rent-control policy for the city and increased affirmative action for both the city and the university. These are all valid issues, but the Berkeley radical left approached them with a sense of moral superiority and political purity that was in some ways reminiscent of the complacent, self-assured leadership of the university and the city in the 1950s. What was different was that the activists who developed this agenda for the "Greening of Berkeley" often regarded themselves as "victims" oppressed by the federal government, by uncaring corporations, and by the most accessible enemy of all, landlords. Their response was, regrettably, to become repressors themselves. The net effect was that radicalism and the greening of Berkeley, rather than letting a "thousand flowers bloom," produced instead new forms of intolerance, particularly for free speech.

Protesters would routinely attempt to stop any event or lecture that did not agree with the radical student or BCA party line of how the world should be. The argument in defense of such tactics became, first, "We have no power, and, even if you listen to us, you won't do what we want." Second, "The moral imperative of the issue is so great that the rules must be suspended, and we are justified in using whatever means are necessary to remove this verbal blight from the Berkeley landscape." Ironically, the ecumenical principle of free speech, twenty years following the FSM, had come to mean only speech that agrees with a radical point of view. In the same way that some students of the 1960s believed that if a subject was hard to learn, it must be improperly taught, so the radicals came to believe that if free speech espouses an idea with which you disagree, it is politically incorrect and must be drowned out or even eliminated.

Even the inauguration of a liberal chancellor, Ira Michael

Heyman, in the Greek Theatre in spring 1981 was continually interrupted by about one hundred antinuclear protesters. As soon as the official party was seated, the protesters began a stream of chants, many of them profane, that drowned out much of what the speakers had to say. Heyman, a man of no small voice, had to shout over the public address system to be heard above the protesters' chant of "Free Speech, Free Speech." At one point Heyman roared he would "be damned" if he'd let the hecklers ruin "the only opportunity I'll ever have to make an inaugural address." On the way back to campus I happened to meet Robert Middlekauff, a professor of American history, who shook his head and said, "Free speech is absolutely necessary, but we certainly paid a high price for it today." This protest had taken place at an outdoor university ceremony that, although official, was not part of the instructional program.

In February 1983, two years after the protests at Heyman's inauguration, a disruption took place during an invited academic lecture by Jeane Kirkpatrick who at that time was serving as United States Ambassador to the United Nations and had been invited by the Berkeley Graduate Division to give the annual Jefferson Lectures on the topic of human rights. This invitation made her an official guest of the Berkeley campus, participating in an academic event that was in many ways an extension of the classroom. She had just returned from El Salvador, where US-supported government troops were battling with guerrilla forces, and she was closely identified with the Reagan administration's Central American foreign policy. She was greeted at Wheeler Auditorium, as were the rest of us, by an overflow audience of 800, a significant number of whom had come to heckle a woman they saw as a willing agent of an immoral US intervention in Central American affairs. The heckling started with deflating of squeaking balloons by about twenty people dressed in black with white makeup so as to look like skeletons. The noise continued with a chanting of "U.S. out of El Salvador" and "Genocide in Guatemala," and went on to "forty-thousand dead." Much of the audience joined in. After twenty minutes of continual interruption, Ambassador Kirkpatrick gave up her attempt to speak on US foreign policy and walked offstage. The moderator, Professor Jesse Choper, who was recently appointed dean of Boalt Hall Law School, after being called Klaus Barbie by the protesters, scolded the audience. "You children ought to be ashamed of yourselves," he said with little effect. Kirkpatrick did not return for about five minutes. During that interval, about half the audience who were doing the heckling had left. Despite my pleading with her at dinner that evening to give the scheduled second lecture under greater security the next day, the ambassador declined. I pointed out that it was important that the university not succumb to mob rule and that she could help us in making a needed statement not only about free speech, but also about academic freedom. I believe that she was personally disposed to stay in order to make this statement, but after several telephone conversations, her staff prevailed, and she left campus. To her Washington colleagues the political expediency of her departure apparently outweighed my arguments to help an embarrassed Berkeley.

We were not prepared for the outburst at the Kirkpatrick lecture. Insufficient police were present, and the university lost control of the event. Because of the costumes, it was impossible to identify the perpetrators for discipline. The regents, many of whom were close to the Reagan administration, were outraged, and the campus was humiliated. In an editorial the next day, the *San Francisco Chronicle* stated,

> It is shameful and ironic that a comparative handful of people prevented Jeane Kirkpatrick, the U.S. Ambassador to the United Nations, from speaking at a forum on human liberty at the University of California campus at Berkeley. Vice Chancellor Roderic Park has reminded the bullies who

disrupted the ambassador's appearance that free speech was once curtailed on the campus and that preventing it today turns our back on the intent of the movement begun at Berkeley 20 years ago.

But this admonishment was too little too late. The unfortunate consequences of political correctness had deeply wounded not only the principle of free speech but also the principle of academic freedom. The event received nationwide coverage. The wound inflicted is still with the Berkeley campus more than twenty-five years later.

Following the Kirkpatrick event, Chancellor Heyman issued a statement in defense of free speech:

...Their (the protesters') lack of tolerance strikes at the very heart of a great university—the free flow of ideas. The right to protest, which is clearly protected under university and campus policies, cannot be confused with the license to prevent the free communication of ideas or to obstruct the free speech rights of speaker and audience. Ample opportunity existed on this campus for those opposed to the visit of Ambassador Kirkpatrick to present speakers on their behalf or to demonstrate peacefully without disrupting her address; an address by the way, which was scholarly and nonpartisan. Campus rules protecting freedom of speech have emerged from widespread consultation and agreement, and I am determined to see that they are observed. Berkeley plays a unique role as a forum for the presence of people representing diverse groups and organizations, and for the free exchange of ideas and exercise of the right to dissent in peaceful fashion. Having carefully reviewed arguments on all sides, I am not convinced by the argument that this right entitles individuals to express their opposition through the intentional disruption of speakers.

I am aware that some try to justify disruption on the basis of the political orientations or viewpoints represented by the speaker. Such an approach is not defensible: ethically, educationally, or legally. Time, place and manner rules governing the conduct at this University are, and must remain, neutral with respect to the content of ideas expressed. They are not based on political, cultural or intellectual popularity contests.

In a presentation in the Academic Senate, Professor Martin Trow identified the special level of concern that arises from disruption of the traditional academic environment of the classroom and lecture hall. Although a limited degree of interruption may be tolerable in open campus "free speech" areas (and even there free speech must be protected), Professor Trow noted,

[I]n our classrooms and lecture halls, and in our invited lectures, we have a different standard of attention and civility: we ordinarily do not accept even mild forms of heckling. We engage in discussions governed in principle by reason and evidence; we are not able to sustain the climate conducive to that kind of exchange in the face of heckling and disrupting. We are, as a university, committed to an intellectual life which is the very opposite of heckling and shouting slogans, and we need a special and protected environment if that kind of discussion is to be carried on—by the faculty, by students, and by invited speakers. In other words, at issue here is not only the principle of free speech but also the more elusive, but equally important concept of academic freedom. This does not require acceptance of a speaker's views but it does require acknowledgment that an academic community can only sustain itself by shared standards of conduct and courtesy....

An important point of Trow's argument was that there are different standards for free speech behavior within the hierarchy of university functions. The different marchers through the university, each with their own totems and taboos, must recognize each other's customs and expectations if the university is to function as an institution. The verbal behavior that accompanies a Sproul Plaza brawl necessarily differs from the linguistic rules of debate that govern the classroom.

Following the Kirkpatrick incident, most of our discussions centered on maintaining security in a campus community that has to be open to all comers. We ticketed events rather than having open admission. We avoided dispensing large blocks of tickets, which would allow large numbers of protesters to assemble in one portion of the lecture hall. We held more events in large closed lecture halls rather than outdoors where security was hard to maintain. We debated, but never implemented, a plan in which every third row of a theater or auditorium would remain unoccupied at controversial lectures to allow a security force access to all members of the audience. Though there were no disruptions following the Kirkpatrick incident, radical belief in political correctness remained. We sponsored many conservative lecturers, such as Admiral Bobby Inman, without incident during this period. But one wonders to what extent the chill imposed by the radical left affected the number of invitations to and acceptances from moderate and conservative speakers at Berkeley over the past several decades.

In retrospect our subsequent discussions on how to address radical interruption of university events treated primarily the symptoms of the problem and not the substance, which was rooted in the beliefs of a large portion of the Berkeley community. Our problem as an administration was how to deal with the political reality: many on the left were prepared to suppress by disruption words they found offensive. Though we attempted to improve this behavior, it was often beyond our ability to do so effectively.

Testing of free speech and its balance with civil behavior was to undergo still more trials. It seems an evolutionary fact that groups of young people are only too ready to taunt each other. This trend, which ranges from mere teasing at its most benign expression, to mindless gang territorial fights at its most extreme, is a tendency that a multicultural society tries to ameliorate, but it will continue to emerge. Whites versus Blacks versus Asians versus Latinos versus Jews versus Middle-Easterners, Left versus Right, heterosexual versus homosexual, and even male versus female generate conflicts, which originate far outside the campus. To some degree they will always exist in an institution, no matter how forcefully principles of tolerance are implemented.

In fall 1988, insulting and allegedly racially based comments directed at some black women undergraduate students from the window of a fraternity house precipitated an angry discussion at Berkeley about whether the incident was isolated or the product of pervasive institutional racism. Similar occurrences throughout the university became so charged that President David Gardner was compelled to draw a policy line for student-student verbal interaction on what was acceptable and what was unacceptable speech on UC campuses. On September 21, 1989, he issued his "Fighting Words" policy. The cover letter to the new policy stated in part:

> The University of California strives to create campuses that foster the values of mutual respect and tolerance and are free from discrimination based on race, ethnicity, sex, religion, sexual orientation, disability and other personal characteristics.
>
> Nothing in this policy is intended to limit the protection of free speech accorded students by law and University policy. The policy recognizes, however, that words can be used in such a way that they no longer express an idea, but rather are used to injure and intimidate, thus undermining the ability of individuals to participate in the University community.

The policy itself stated that use of fighting words, a concept from the 1942 Supreme Court decision on Chaplinsky vs. New Hampshire, was a violation of university rules subject to disciplinary proceedings. Fighting words were defined as follows:

> [T]hose personally abusive epithets which, when directly addressed to any ordinary person are, in the context used and as a matter of common knowledge, inherently likely to provoke a violent reaction whether or not they actually do so. Such words include, but are not limited to, those terms widely recognized to be derogatory references to race, ethnicity, religion, sex, sexual orientation, disability and other personal characteristics. "Fighting words" constitute "harassment" when the circumstances of their utterance create a hostile and intimidating environment which the student uttering them should reasonably know will interfere with the victim's ability to pursue effectively his or her education or otherwise to participate fully in University programs and activities.

While the policy spoke of students uttering the fighting words to each other, it tactfully avoided the possible use of fighting words by faculty members in the course of their teaching. It was not long before this circumstance would arise, and the university would have to balance free speech protection with the academic freedom of a faculty member in the classroom.

In fall 1990, Berkeley's alumni magazine, the *Cal Monthly*, published an article by Professor Vincent Sarich, an anthropologist with controversial views on human evolution. Sarich was also a vigorous critic of the campus freshman admission policy, expressing a view that subsequently prevailed. Half the admissions to the freshman class at Berkeley at that time were color blind, culture blind, and socioeconomically blind. An algorithm using the highest grades and test scores in required high school courses was the only criterion used in these admission decisions. Except for the fact that out-of-state students were limited to no more than 14 percent of the freshman class, the first tier of admissions was a formulaic meritocracy by traditional standards. The second tier also consisted of students in the top 12.5 percent of graduating high school seniors statewide, but additional criteria including race were used in the admission decision, with the objective of matriculating a diverse class. This method, while now prohibited, was then consistent with regental, state, and faculty guidelines.

In the *Cal Monthly* article, Sarich disagreed with this policy, and asserted that UC Berkeley admission policies "have systematically, and increasingly, discriminated against white students and institutionalized racism on our campus." This article, plus his reputation for controversial opinions (which include the possibility that brain size may influence intelligence, that race may influence ability, and that heterosexuality is "more natural") led to disruption of his class by seventy-five protesters on November 7, 1990. Reflecting on that confrontation, we can see that, in a perverse way, each side got what it wanted. A provocative professor received publicity, and the radical students had a target for their anger. Only the university was the loser, as the media and the Academic Senate decried the loss of forums for intellectual debate at the university. Protests at the Anthropology Department, or outside Wheeler Hall Auditorium where the class was offered to 400 students, would have met the standards of our academic culture, but disruption of a class was, is, and will remain an academic taboo of the most serious sort. The classroom of a major university is not a street corner, a fact lost on the culture of intolerant political correctness.

Profound questions emerge from the confrontation between the moral certainty of the espousers of political correctness and those defending academic freedom on the lecture podium and in the classroom. Is the fighting-words argument, currently limited to student-student interaction, also applicable to student-faculty interactions? Does academic freedom in a forum of non-equals—students and faculty—have a limit when it diminishes students' self-worth? If a policy governing such limits were in place, what would be the process for determining whether infractions had occurred and, if they had, how could sanctions ever be enforced given the substantial protections awarded the faculty under the Faculty Code of Conduct? These are complicated questions of the second kind. They balance the rights of students with the academic freedom and rights of faculty members. It is an area that is perhaps better handled by common sense than detailed regulation and process.

These examples demonstrate an important distinction in the standards applied to first amendment rights. By trial and error and by judicial decisions, first amendment standards have become adapted to a wide range of university activities. The standards for free speech protection in an outdoor debate in Sproul Plaza are little more than the physical protection of the antagonists, and noise suppression to the extent that classes and other offices are not interrupted during working hours. The next level of activity is the large sporting event, such as a football or basketball game, where cheering and shouting down the other rooters have become part of the contest. A third level is an official, quasi-academic university function, such as colloquia held in the Greek Theater. On these occasions, protesters interfering with the ceremony are likely to be escorted out of the meeting but are unlikely to have charges pressed against them. Should a colloquium be held in an indoor auditorium, the standard for free speech on the part of the protesters becomes somewhat higher than it was in the Greek Theater, because it becomes easier to disrupt the ceremony in an indoor space. Progressively higher standards are held for invited lectures, and the highest standard of all is maintained for the official instructional program itself.

These distinctions are not easily accepted by an absolutist mind whether from the Right or the Left. To the morally pure and politically correct, complexity is mere waffling! There are other laws whose standards for enforcement are also based on location. Speed limits, for example, are more strictly enforced at elementary schools than on desert highways in Nevada. First amendment rights appear unique in their restrictions as defined by different sociological settings.

During the fall semester of 1990, Dinesh D'Sousa, author of *Illiberal Education: The Politics of Race and Sex on Campus,* and critic of Berkeley admissions policies and curricular changes, gave a public lecture on the Berkeley campus. There was no protest. The audience was polite while asking searching, difficult questions. If political correctness leading to disruption was a goal secretly desired by some on the Right, they were disappointed. The marchers at Berkeley were regaining their equilibrium.

Other Student Parades

Though the students who emerge through student political processes such as the student government and student political movements are often radical, and often limited in their interests to a few issues, they are a minority. The student government at Berkeley is officially called the Associated Students University of California or ASUC. Generally only about 20 percent of the eligible students vote in ASUC elections, 10 percent of the students actually voting for the winning party. Thus the ASUC never has a broad political base, but it is the student government, and the administration deals with it as the legitimate voice of students.

Following the student protests of the 1960s, several minority ASUC governments were elected by what was then a predominately Caucasian student body. One might assume that these students were lineal descendants of the radical movements of the '60s, but this was not the case. In retrospect, these ASUC officers, for the most part, were supportive of the institution and did not attack its central educational purpose. The minority students, especially the Blacks, were more "streetwise" than their Caucasian counterparts, and wanted mostly "their piece of the action" in recruitment programs and sponsored events. Their demands could be dealt with, and looking back they were benign compared with the confrontations that followed when in the late 1970s the Caucasian students again took control of the ASUC. The new Caucasian officers were much more radical than the minority governments had been, and were quite prepared to attack the central intellectual mission of the university as racist in its orientation and in need of reconstitution. These students developed an effective student lobby, which for a time in the early 1980s was regarded as one of the most effective lobbies in Sacramento. They demanded equivalent student participation in governance for all decisions made by the university, from the granting of faculty tenure to monitoring the content of courses and participating in budgetary decisions. There were some legislators in Sacramento who supported the student lobby in this program. One used to say in effect that "in the old world we were all born sinful and knew that it took such institutions as the church and the university to save us. Now we know that, at worst, we are born innocent and it is these very institutions which stand in our way!"

In the late 1970s we had, for a time, an annual student retreat with about twenty-five students and five to ten administrators including the chancellor, four vice chancellors, two provosts, and the graduate dean. The meetings became increasingly confrontational. Each of ten or fifteen students had been coached to attack the motives and morality of the institution on a different issue, from roles in governance to lack of effective affirmative action in student, faculty, and staff ranks. Whatever had been accomplished by the institution was only evidence of administrative incapacity, whereas the student government emerged as the oppressed moral core of a corrupt institution.

These meetings served as an initiation rite for new student officers who would prove their right to their jobs by fearlessly attacking a feckless administration. Since these meetings were destructive, they were terminated as a formal event. Instead, before the fall semester the chancellor would meet with the main student officers at his home to discuss the process for addressing issues of concern to them over the ensuing academic year. In recent years student political parties have found it to their advantage to run ethnically balanced slates of student officers, a practice that lessened confrontation and benefited both the students and the institution.

As Dean of the College of Letters and Science, to obtain additional student views and values, I asked the undergraduate organizations in each of the forty departments of the college to elect a representative for a "Dean's Student Consulting Group" to identify and work with me on issues of mutual concern. Our first meeting was a refreshing change. The students were primarily academic in their orientation. They had been picked by their peers, not for their radical postures, but because they were among the academic elite in the department and because they strongly desired to maintain and improve the academic quality of their units. They became a source of students to serve on departmental review committees, conducted their own studies, and most of all, gave me reassurance that most students held deep affection for their institution.

A second group of students who emerged as curators and improvers of Berkeley were those who served on the ASUC-sponsored Student Fee Committee. This committee advised me as the vice chancellor on the expenditure of over $40,000,000 generated each year for student services. These funds were derived from fees paid by students, and were restricted by regental policy to student service units such as the Counseling Center, the Student Learning Center, the Student Health Service, recreational sports programs, intercollegiate athletics, campus cultural programs, the University Art Museum, and a host of other programs, including a portion for student financial aid.

When I was assigned this group of students in 1980, the process was highly politicized, and I was regarded as someone not to trust. The distrust, which was obviously mutual, was born out of a style of administration in which control had been exerted by selectively dispensing financial information. The students were not receiving unequal treatment—they were being treated exactly like other administrative units and departments. The Berkeley campus had run this way for many years, and many bureaucracies still do.*

I was able to reverse the students' paranoia totally in two or three years. My first rule was "If you are going to make people responsible, give them responsibility." Give the students the data and support, and take them seriously, with the understanding that you will not always agree, but will let them know why and respect their opinions. I also prevailed on their emerging sense of professionalism as they aspired to gain entry to professional graduate schools. They became proud of their role, and took on a sense of proprietorship for these programs and the distribution of resources among them. They defended necessary but unpopular decisions with the student constituencies when fee increases were insufficient to cover increases in program costs and cuts had to be made. Before members of the Student Fee Committee graduated, they often asked me to write them letters of recommendation. Because of their new stewardship they were easy to support. In the beginning this student parade had been part of the problem. Over the years these same students became part of the solution.

---

* BX (Before Xerox), the breadth of decision making was restricted by the fact that the typewriter produced only two legible carbon copies, and therefore very few people made most decisions. The ability to quickly produce fifty copies of a proposal produced a more inclusive management style, much to the discomfort of many traditionalists.

If it is improper to consider the faculty as monolithic, it is more so for the students. There are not two or three student stereotypes at UC Berkeley or CU Boulder, but hundreds. Because of the many different agendas that interest these groups, in the absence of a major crisis it is unlikely that there will be more large "student movements" at Berkeley in the foreseeable future. But the students will, and indeed must, continue to question both institutional authority and society's assumptions if they are, first, to become educated, and second, to become effective and contributing citizens.

All students of a university, like it or not, march on to become alumni. Almost invariably, alumni feel their greatest allegiance to the college they attended as undergraduates. Graduate students are more directed toward a narrow discipline, have friends who are studying in the same areas, and do not have the time or interest to explore the wider community of the university. Undergraduates have more time and more inclination for collegiate high jinks, sports, dances, and club or fraternity life, activities that often lead to an enduring memory of the excitement and the limitless potential of youth that they continue to associate with their alma mater. Alumni in later years, because of their love for the role that their university played in their lives, become the university's greatest supporters and benefactors.

Graduation is not a prerequisite for joining most alumni associations. One has only to attend an institution (even a summer session will do), and solicitation for donations and membership in the alumni association will soon follow. If the degree-less student becomes very successful and supportive of the university in later life, he or she may look forward eventually to receiving a degree (honorary of course), even though unqualified for the BA.*

---

* An apocryphal story about President Robert Gordon Sproul recounts that during the depression, as a quid pro quo for a large gift from a degree-less alumnus who bred racehorses, President Sproul agreed to award an honorary

The university's most important product is people. It is the institution's graduates who provide the vast majority of knowledge and technical transfer from the university to the larger society. Alumni, in turn, are the most important constituency for any older university fortunate to have graduates of all ages throughout the fabric of society. Alumni, through the positions they hold, will always be one of the university's greatest sources of political and financial support.

---

degree to the breeder's best stallion. He is reputed to have said when making the award, "Ladies and Gentlemen, by authority vested in me by the Regents and the State Constitution, I am about to do something never before done in North American Higher Education. I am about to award an honorary degree to an entire horse!"

Chapter 5

The President: Leading through Mediation

It is no fun running a university these days.
— Arthur M. Schlesinger Jr.

The university president[*] is a focal point for concerns from inside and outside the institution. Whether the issue is raising tuition, recovering overhead on federal grants and contracts, or maintaining academic standards for college athletes, it is ultimately the president, with the support of trustees or regents, who must explain the programs of the university and its needs to the larger public and to the campus. In turn, the president must adapt the institution to changing political and economic circumstances of the real world while keeping its academic integrity intact. This adaptation must be accomplished in the face of increasing demands upon all universities, and particularly public universities, for increased accountability and sensitive response to one-issue groups. We should not be surprised that the average tenure of a university president is now less than seven years,

---

[*] The titles "president" and "chancellor" are sometimes used interchangeably. The head of the University of California is a president. The head of the California State University is a chancellor. Here, president refers to the head of a system or private institution.

and that more than 300 institutions of higher education in the United States are searching at any one time for that "right person" who can lead them through what their governing boards often perceive as unique problems.

One way to understand the role of a college president as we embark on the twenty-first century is to answer a question that I was often asked as the vice chancellor at Berkeley: "What is the difference between the job of the chief academic officer and the president of a campus?" The answer is embedded in the fact that 140 years ago the jobs were identical, and one person generally did both. President Charles William Eliot of Harvard, for example, hired and fired faculty and was the primary architect of both a changing curriculum and the emerging departmental structure at Harvard. At the same time, he was campus spokesman to the outside world of alumni and the public as well as the primary fundraiser, a role that has not changed. But the president's role as the central academic and administrative architect for the campus in addition to being spokesperson for the university has changed since Eliot's time and particularly during the past five decades. The outside world is now more vocal and demands much greater accountability than it did fifty years ago. Research universities have announced to the public, and the public in turn has come to believe, that universities are steppingstones to a more satisfying and rewarding life for anyone who is qualified to attend. For places like the University of California at Berkeley or the University of Colorado at Boulder, where many more applicants are qualified to attend than can be admitted, the fairness of the access criteria are constantly questioned. Both a national sympathy for exercise of civil rights, which is now extended to almost all individual rights, not only of people but also of animals, and the emerging roles of television and the Internet as the chief purveyors of news in the United States have thrust universities onto the center stage of changing values among the young, a stage on which their elders see their greatest hopes and worst fears coming to pass. Given these cascading demands and increasing financial stringency demanding greatly increased efforts in fundraising, presidents have delegated much of their former academic responsibility to their chief academic officers who may hold any of the following titles: Provost, Executive Vice Chancellor, Vice Chancellor for Academic Affairs, or Vice President for Academic Affairs. This title ambiguity is a constant source of confusion.

In the midst of these unfolding dramas, today's university presidents often find themselves directing plays, often reruns of past bad ones, which for the most part present more perils than upside possibilities to the institution. Competing external groups want the university to vindicate and certify their views and political goals by agreeing with them; universities have responded, usually because they are legally required to do so. But sometimes they respond excessively. For example, the non-discrimination statement of the University of California might just have said, "The University of California does not discriminate illegally." Instead it lists seventeen separate categories of illegal discrimination. In 2006 these were race, color, national origin, religion, sex (including sexual harassment), gender identity, pregnancy/childbirth and medical conditions related thereto, disability, age, medical condition (cancer related), ancestry, marital status, citizenship, sexual orientation or transgender status, or status as a Vietnam era veteran or special disabled veteran. To be so specifically recognized by institutional policy is one ambition of every new university interest group.

The president must carefully weave among these many contentious issues. An example was the debate twenty years ago over the policies that a university should follow with respect to endowments invested in corporations that do business with the Republic of South Africa. An immediate desire for a university moral posture by the students, some faculty members, and outside groups was directly opposed by the fiduciary posture of trustees in many institutions. The president was at the center, attempting to invoke reason when not reason, but passion, was the currency of the camps the president was attempting to reconcile. Issues such as affirmative action for admissions and hiring of faculty and staff, animal experimentation in research, and privacy-based protection of a homosexual lifestyle are all examples of contentious issues where presidents have attempted to steer their institutions by the paths of reason rather than accommodating the passions of opposing constituencies.

The result is that successful presidents have become masters at dealing with ambiguity. Their job is to reconcile and accommodate the many interests buffeting the university, and starve rather than feed the incipient polarizations among them.[*]

This skill is best observed when the president is asked a clear and pointed question on a difficult issue, preferably in a public setting. The question might start with an observation: "You have spent the past twenty minutes telling us about your great need for financial contributions from the alumni." Then it goes on: "Isn't it true that professorial teaching loads are 30 percent less than they were only thirty years ago? You don't need money, you need management. What are you going to do about that?"

The university president's answering style is best compared to lifting a figurine enclosed in a crystal ball from the shelf of a gift shop. The question is initially as clear and as pointed as the figure itself. The president proceeds to twirl the ball and start a snowstorm in which the question all but disappears. Over the several minutes that it takes to answer the question, the snow slowly settles, leaving a barely recognizable snow-clad figure. The question is now buried in the soft whiteness of ambiguity

---

[*] President Lawrence Summers of Harvard failed to follow this rule to his chagrin. He recently suggested at an economic conference that there might be "innate differences" between men and women that explain why there are relatively fewer women in math and the sciences than in, say, the humanities. He apparently forgot there is a difference between being a university president and a talk show host!

and, whereas snow shovels might be in order, the beauty of the scene lulls the audience on to the next question.

The president must become passably acquainted with another side of the university, particularly important to some alumni: sports. Sports are important, if for no other reason than they provide one of the few occasions when all segments of the institution come together as a community. It is often mistakenly believed that intercollegiate athletics generate financial profits for a campus. In most universities, intercollegiate athletic expenses considerably exceed the revenue they generate. Especially for those institutions very dependent on tuition income, sports are an important source of publicity, which helps admissions. Unfortunately, however, each year brings evidence that "big-time" collegiate sports also carry risks. Income from televised sports events in some universities has produced programs that are largely alumni-subsidized farm teams, particularly for professional football franchises who return nothing to their benefactors. Financial operations on this scale can and will corrupt. No president should become too identified with a big-time sports program, because there is always the potential for scandals, and where this is an expected hazard for the coaches, the president is held to a higher standard.

The chief academic officer (CAO), a role I played for eight years at Berkeley, is also a political animal, but the CAO deals with more limited constituencies. This person is usually the lever arm that implements program changes within the institution. Because universities are collegial in nature, the CAO becomes the internal tactician, not only for leading the students and faculty to water, but also for making them think it is their own idea. Asking a question of a chief academic officer does not generally stop with a snowstorm. Faculty members are well armed with snow shovels! Knowing this, the CAO behaves more like the leader of a bucket brigade while the president serves as the campus lookout scanning the distant horizon for fires.

Beyond being a good manager and making good appointments, there are two principal components of presidential leadership. The first is obvious and well understood—the knowledge and political acumen to make the right decisions most of the time, and to recognize when decisions are not correct and to modify them and recover. But a second part of decision making is likely to be more important than the first: the ability to legitimize the decisions made to the point that one has sufficient political support to govern. What an institution needs to lead it is a person who, through personal ability or the recruitment of capable advisors, brings both qualities to bear on institutional life: the ability to make good decisions and the ability to gain broad enough support for them so that institutional movement and progress are possible. People who are quick at good decision making but who do not have the political skill to legitimize their decisions are almost always people who cannot live with ambiguity.

Practical Application: My First Day as a Chancellor

My first contact with the Boulder campus occurred in 1941 when my mother, a graduate of the Greeley Teachers College, took my sister and me to visit the University of Colorado at Boulder (CU), in her words "a real college." We were on a summer trip west to visit my grandmother, Edith Turner, herself a pioneer from the Ferris Mountains in Wyoming. We parked next to "Old Main," and my mother went into this first building on the Boulder campus and emerged with a course catalogue. We then sat under a tree as she explained various departments and what they taught. As we wound our way back to Greeley there was an intense hailstorm, which forced us to abandon the '41 Ford and seek shelter in a roadside café. I remember thinking at the time that Boulder was a very rural and remote place.

My second contact with Boulder occurred fifty-three years

later in January 1994. David Wynn, the chair of the CU Board of Regents, asked if I would join a team of consultants to review a structural study of the university. This study was done in response to an incident in which the academic vice chancellor and some deans from Boulder had confronted the new president of the University of Colorado, Judith Albino, and demanded her resignation. What had started out nominally by the Boulder administrators as a trip to President Albino's office evolved into a six-hour public confrontation involving regents, local television, and public relations advisors. This public confrontation, although exciting theater, brought little distinction to the university or confidence in its administration. Colorado regents are not appointed by the governor, as in most states, but are elected as Republicans and Democrats at the bottom of the ticket. While democratic, this method of selection does not always assure that candidates are thoroughly vetted. The structural study that ensued was actually a euphemism for some serious administrative dislocations at the University of Colorado.

To serve as a consultant under these circumstances sounded like a job worthy of someone who cleans up problems—the academic "janitor" described in chapter 8. Our team made three visits to Denver and Boulder. During this time the CU president was surviving on a 5 to 4 vote of the regents, and the Boulder chancellor was scheduled to leave his post by the end of June. Our final visit occurred in May, and culminated in a large meeting at the Denver Medical School where we gave our conclusions and answered questions. Colorado is an exceptionally polite place compared with Berkeley, and though we gave direct and often unsympathetic answers to the questions from regents, faculty, students, and staff, voices were never raised.

Not until several months later did I discover what strong politics run under this polite veneer. When my final flight took off from Stapleton Airport to San Francisco, I had the same feeling that one had on an airplane leaving Moscow during the Cold

War: often there was applause as the plane left Russian soil. I thought no more about my Boulder visit until the telephone rang one month later and a regental staff member from CU asked if I would consider being a candidate for an interim chancellor position at Boulder, as the incumbent was not continuing. When asked a question such as this, never respond immediately. Say instead, "Let me think about that; I will get back to you." To answer immediately either yes or no shows the questioner you are impetuous or not very thoughtful. After consulting my wife, Cathy, I called back. I said I was interested, though I did not add that my interest stemmed from my knowledge of their fine faculty and that things were such a mess. How could I fail? The job was a challenge that would test every skill I had acquired—and I could not make things much worse. As of August 1, 1994 I was in Boulder as Interim Chancellor of the Boulder Campus of the University of Colorado. Not until two years later did I discover that of five candidates for this job, I had been ranked number 5 by the president, but number 1 by the faculty leadership. The faculty had prevailed, but my tenure in this job would be a tumultuous one. Had I known my low ranking by the president before accepting the offer, it would not have changed my decision to take it.

While driving to Boulder in our Ford Ranger, Cathy and I stopped in Wyoming for breakfast and read a feature article in the *Denver Post* about the current CU football coach, Bill McCartney, who was reputed to have more name recognition in Colorado than the governor. I reviewed his football success, lesser success with events in his family, and the role of religious commitments in his life.

This all came into focus the next day, my first day on the job as interim chancellor. Before arriving at work at 8:00 a.m. I had read through four newspapers at a Pearl Street cafe in Boulder, paying particular attention to the letters to the editor concerning CU. Among the items, the *Boulder Daily Camera* had published a photograph on the lower right of its first page showing a freshman fullback recruit from Detroit looking for housing with his parents. Not much news here until 10:00 a.m. when the director of admissions knocked on my door. "Chancellor," he said, "Did you see that photograph on the first page of the *Daily Camera?*" He went on, "Chancellor, that student was never admitted." So, first day on the job and I was being challenged by someone with more name recognition than the governor. And being from California I was already branded as an outsider of the worst kind, a "Californicator!"

I called the Athletic Director, Bill Marolt, and instructed him to bring Bill McCartney to meet with me at 4:00 p.m. We sat at the end of a table in the chancellor's office and I said I understood that this recruit who was in Boulder had not been admitted. What was going on? What followed was a ten-minute soliloquy by the coach on how he knew the parents; how he knew the councilors; how he knew the pastors; how he had visited the recruits in their own homes, and how he knew who should be admitted to CU. About halfway through this speech it became apparent to me that he had engaged in conversations with powers far greater than those held by earthly beings, and that I was in all probability dealing with divine intervention. I responded, "It is too late to get to the bottom of this. You have me this time, and I will admit the recruit by special action, but here is what I am extracting from you: I am appointing a commission of faculty members and alumni to review the entire record of your special-action admissions for the past five years including how many students completed their degrees and how many left and for what reasons. You may be assured I will take their recommendations very seriously." By the end of that fall semester Coach McCartney had resigned, and the star recruit returned to Detroit without having posted a single passing grade at Boulder. Following that first day there were many more such "surprises." The janitorial challenges exceeded even those I imagined.

Also in my first day on the Boulder campus I was named, with the former chancellor, as a coconspirator in a sexual harassment suit by a staff member in the chancellor's office. Though I was eventually dropped as a defendant, my first few hours as a chancellor reemphasized a continuing need for "janitorial" skills under an umbrella of ambiguity!

Dealing with such first-day incidents is never covered in "chancellor school." You call on your inner values and common sense in such circumstances. Continuing sports scandals and free speech issues since I left CU twelve years ago speak eloquently to the turbulent waters in which that fine university finds itself. When will the citizens of Colorado learn that there is life beyond football, that there are more important issues than serving beer in the stadium, and that certain faculty members, such as Ward Churchill, would rather be vilified than neglected?

Chapter 6

Academic and Staff Employees

Oh wad some Power the giftie gie us
To see oursels as ithers see us.
— Robert Burns (1759–1796)

The university employs two different systems for promoting and rewarding individuals who work for it. These two groups are academic employees; that is, those who teach and do research, and staff employees, those who support the primary teaching and research functions of a university.

Academic employees consist of the regular ladder faculty members, who either have tenure or are in apprenticeship status as assistant professors. These individuals compose the academic senate. Non-tenure-track academic employees include the lecturers, who are usually hired as temporary and often part-time teachers, the graduate-student instructors or teaching assistants, and the tutors and readers. Also included are the graduate-student research assistants, laboratory assistants, laboratory technicians, staff research assistants, and some other titles. Compensation ranges are defined for each title and increased experience can be rewarded over time even if the job description is unchanged.

Staff employees, the clerical, professional, and middle and upper management groups, are hired according to the pay and classification system. Their promotions are defined by the demands of their job descriptions, how many people and how much budget they supervise, and the extent to which they apply independent decision making to their respective duties. This same pay and classification system applies to all such workers employed by the state of California.

These two different employment systems exist side by side in each department, and if not understood, lead to unnecessary tension, particularly among the clerical staff who sense they are a less privileged class of employees.

Academic Employees

Salary steps in tenured academic titles, movement from one step to higher ones in the series, do not involve a change in job descriptions, only continued excellent performance. In ladder faculty tenure ranks, the job description of an assistant professor is identical with that of a Nobel laureate, though the latter receives four or five times the salary of the former. Faculty members are expected to do teaching, research, and public service in an increasingly sophisticated way throughout their university careers, and are accordingly increased in salary in relation to their continuing accomplishments. A similar relationship exists among the non-tenured teaching and research ranks, except that there is some financial recognition of greater supervisory responsibility for researchers.

Non-tenure Ranks: Lecturers and Graduate Student Instructors

Many university towns acquire a group of citizens that are a product of the institution's failures. It is true that most students who attend the university enjoy, or at least tolerate, their years there, receive their degrees, and move on to other jobs and careers. But some, particularly among the graduate students, for a variety of reasons from money to motivation, never finish their theses and become academic casualties. For many of these casualties, dropping out of graduate study does not mean rejection of the intellectual life. The exciting politics of a university town, the bohemian character of the university, and the atmosphere surrounding the young indicating that all things are possible, prove irresistible. Whereas about 75 percent of the undergraduate students who matriculate at Berkeley eventually receive their degrees, the success rate among graduate students who are candidates for the doctoral degree is much lower. In the humanities, in particular, the average time to degree is long, over ten years in the philosophy department. The opportunities for financial support are few. The number of graduate students in the humanities, with its paucity of federal and industry support, vastly exceeds the number of teaching assistantships or research positions available, so many doctoral students must work and thus become part-time degree candidates. After five years of survival, candidates find that they are twenty-seven years old, five years away from a degree, and in 2008 making a maximum of $32,800 per year as teaching assistants. In addition, they are not assured of a job in a research institution when they finally do graduate, and may spend the rest of their lives at the salary scale of a community college or high school. It is not surprising that many elect to "drop out" of graduate school, somewhat embittered, but often still in love with the intellectual life and promise of a university.

Many of these former graduate students, whether or not they finally attain their degrees, decide to continue at the university as employees. Though generally "overqualified," they obtain jobs as administrative assistants, accountants, museum curators, and in various technical areas. They continue to live in the rent-controlled housing they occupied as students, and to participate in the cultural life of the university. But some also house resentment against the university—resentment stemming from their belief that they might have become faculty members at a university had fate been kinder. In addition, this cadre of former graduate students that inhabit university towns, whose talents often exceed by a considerable margin the jobs in which they are working, provides an almost inexhaustible number of lecturers to teach courses on a temporary basis. These are often courses that the regular faculty is either too busy or too bored to teach. In a 1970 UC Berkeley report, "An Economic Theory of Ph.D. Production: The Case At Berkeley," David W. Breneman maintained that the structure of many foreign language departments was actually designed to produce this dismal result in doctoral-student success rates in order to maintain faculty prerogatives. An excerpt from this report follows:

> Consider first the economy of the French department. Previously it was suggested that the demand for Ph.D.'s in French is not great and has been reasonably stable during the last several years, relative to many other disciplines. It was argued that this fact explains the low success rate in French. Weakness in the market also explains the lack of financial support available to graduate students of French. The department, however, has a demand for graduate students based on its need to produce student credit hours [see p. 29] to maintain its claim over university resources. Furthermore, the presence of numerous graduate students generates demand for advanced courses in highly specialized areas of French Literature, the type of courses that faculty members like to teach. The department's demand for graduate students coupled with the minimal demand for French Ph.D.'s would pose a serious problem were it not for the presence of Letters and Science undergraduates who are required to complete four quarters of a foreign language. This requirement generates a large demand for teaching assistants and solves the department's problem of

providing financial support for graduate students. Thus, the economy of this department rests, somewhat perilously, on the demand for undergraduate instruction artificially created by breadth requirements.

The technology of Ph.D. production in this field is reasonably simple and, from the department's point of view, inexpensive. Faculty input is limited to course offerings, testing, and thesis advising; capital requirements are classroom space and library facilities, provided by university funds. The department has no incentive to economize on the use of resources required to provide Ph.D.'s; in fact, there is every incentive to maximize use and control over such resources.

From the perspective of the French faculty, then, the graduate student must be viewed as a very valuable member of the department's economy. Not only does the graduate student teach the dull introductory courses, but he is a source of student credit hours and demand for advanced instruction. Departmental technology is such that having graduate students in residence for several years is costless to the faculty, and not without certain advantages. First, the experienced teaching assistant requires minimal supervision; if graduate turnover were high, faculty would be forced to spend more time working with the fledgling teachers. In addition, second and third year graduates can be expected to enroll in more advanced courses, thereby allowing increased faculty specialization. Consequently, in this type of department, faculty members have no incentives to make rapid decisions to terminate Ph.D. aspirants. Graduate students are particularly valuable assets to such departments, and will be kept in residence as long as possible. Eventually, fatigue, financial pressures, or the dissertation will produce the necessary attrition.

Linking the analysis of the first part with the above, we have a picture of a humanities department desiring a high attrition rate, but not wanting this to occur within the early years of the student's graduate career. If this is an accurate description of the department's objectives, we would expect to find the following features of the graduate program:

1. Critical hurdles designed to eliminate candidates in the late rather than in the early stages of the program.

2. A curriculum sufficiently ambiguous and fuzzy to keep students mildly confused about their rate of progress toward the degree.

3. Conscious minimization of the student's feeling that he is a member of a particular graduate class or cohort. A student should have a minimum of checkpoints by which to measure his progress.

4. Feedback from the department designed to keep the student's estimate of success high.

5. Extremely demanding requirements for the dissertation, this being the final hurdle for the degree.

6. Use of the same individuals as teaching assistants for several years.

7. Absence of discussion or information related to the job market for Ph.D.'s

8. A general lack of information about the historical success rates of graduate students, attrition patterns, and so forth. The best policy for the department would be to minimize information flows to the students.

9. A tendency for the department not to keep detailed records on the experience of past graduate students.

10. Little evidence of major curriculum revisions.

Given that this analysis was often true in the humanities disciplines, it is not surprising that there was a constant drive for unionization among some graduate student employees who found themselves in departments where they were treated as second-class citizens and where they were exploited in terms of the kinds of courses they taught and the workloads they carried. The drive for formal union affiliation and recognition among the graduate-student teaching assistants in the early days was a particularly vexing problem for the University of California because it was not clear whether graduate-student roles as teaching assistants were part of their graduate training or whether they were in fact employees of the institution performing a service beyond the requirements of their graduate degrees.* This issue came before the California courts for clarification of the intent of the California Higher Education Employee Relations Act with respect to graduate-student employees. To observers like myself, it was evident that after four semesters of teaching the same or similar courses, in the languages, for example, graduate-student teaching assistants move past their learning stage and begin to fill the role of teaching employees of the university. This view was eventually adopted by the courts, and graduate student instructors are now a recognized bargaining unit.

The availability of unsuccessful graduate students (either because they dropped out or, if they obtained their graduate degree, because they were unable to find an acceptable job at another university) for service as staff and lecturer positions leads some faculty members to equate many staff members with

---

* Unionization of graduate-student employees was forestalled for about ten years once health insurance was made available. Initial plans assumed that, for the insurance plan to succeed, graduate student enrollment would be mandatory. I observed, "You can't use the 'M' word at Berkeley." The staff then substituted the phrase "automatically enrolled" and the graduate students approved!

failed students. This exacerbates the status differences between regular tenure faculty and staff and temporary faculty, which exist in many universities—a difference in which some faculty members perceive the staff as menial servants and not as professional assistants. Faculty members holding these views generally lack any managerial experience and do not appreciate the role of morale in an institution or how to use it. Fortunately they are balanced by many others on the faculty whose exposure to larger societal responsibilities has been greater and who understand the role of leadership in maintaining productive institutions that command best efforts from all their members.

Staff Employees

Often, faculty members called to administrative duties such as departmental chair are unaware that the staff members they now supervise are rewarded differently from themselves and their faculty colleagues. This leads to tension between the new faculty administrators and the personnel office because new department chairs often apply faculty experience and believe their staff, like faculty, should be promoted for continuing good service. When the personnel office rejects the new chair's requests because the staff candidate is still doing the same job, the new chair is often mystified and angered.

A particular problem for staff members in academic departments is their difficulty in acquiring sufficient independent decision-making authority for promotion and advancement under the pay and classification system. Faculty members, by nature, are reluctant to see decision making of all but the most routine sort pass into the hands of nonacademic staff. As a result, the staff in academic departments, even with large support budgets and many employees, hold lower paying jobs than their counterparts in comparably sized and budgeted units in the accounting, telecommunications, or other large administrative offices. This trend was countered somewhat by the unionization of clerical staff. The rules of employment contracts developed under collective bargaining became so complex that, in their attempts at supervision, amateur faculty-department chairs ran the constant risk of incurring charges of unfair labor practices. This forced the chairs to give greater authority to their chief staff person in employee supervision and grievance matters, thus increasing their responsibilities.

In one case, further delegation of authority to staff was caused by the academic complexity of a department itself. The Anthropology Department, like its counterparts throughout the United States, contains a range of research interests that exceeds that of any other academic unit. There are, to be sure, traditional cultural anthropologists and museum curators, but other faculty interests range as far afield as folklorists, psychologists, and those who study comparative literature. There are archaeologists who work in periods from recent history to those who study pre-cultural primate evolution and the campsites of early hominids. And finally there are primatologists most interested in 3–4 million-year-old hominid remains and footprints from the Afar Triangle of Ethiopia. Thus anthropology departments have become universities within universities, and the interaction of faculty members at the university level among departments, which ranges from cooperation to indifference and jealousy, is now all encompassed within one academic unit. The great range of academic interests and competition for resources (faculty positions, space, and support budget within the department) makes anthropology governance at the departmental level a significant challenge. Would the primate archaeologists be satisfied that a folklorist chair could understand and respect their priorities? Probably not. Thus the Anthropology Department has evolved a unique governance structure. Instead of a department chair, anthropology is governed by a committee of three faculty members, representing the major academic areas, one of whom is designated as the secretary and convener. This assures department members that all groups will be heard and all initiatives will be vetted. This diffuse structure and the attending difficulty of making timely departmental management decisions has left much decision making in the hands of the chief staff person in the department. As a consequence, this individual has more responsibility and decision-making authority than any other chief staff member in the College of Letters and Science, and is therefore classified a full step higher than the others.

Those in the university, either academic or staff employees, who are not in tenured series always feel they are in a lower caste. Unlike industry, where there is more of a continuum among jobs, in the university there is a discontinuity that distinguishes an "elite" that is differentiated from all other professions, the tenure-track positions. When this discontinuity is treated responsibly by the tenured elite, it is not a barrier to the smooth conduct of business. On the other hand, thoughtless elitism is always a formula for trouble, more often than not in the form of union intervention. It took the insight of Plato to appreciate that faculty elitism, if it becomes too separated from the real world, has its downside risks.

> *"Any one of us might say, that although in words he is not able to meet you at each step of the argument, he sees in fact that academic persons when they carry on study, not only in youth as part of their education, but as the pursuit of their maturer years, most of them become decidedly queer, not to say rotten; and that those who may be considered the best of them are made useless to the world by the very study which you extol.*
>
> *"Well, do you think that those who say so are wrong?"*
>
> *"I cannot tell," he replied; "but I should like to know what is your opinion?"*

*"Hear my answer; I am of the opinion
that they are quite right."*
— Plato, *Republic VI**

Most staff members in the university have a great love for the institution, often as much or more than the faculty members who are the main determinants of institutional programs and directions. Staff members usually lack the career mobility of tenured faculty, and regard the university as a home in which they grew up. They deal with the everyday details as well as with specialized support, which allows us, the faculty, in Cornford's words, "to enjoy the contemplation of truth" without the vexations and distractions of day-to-day responsibilities. When academic administrators discover this, their admiration for their staff will not only increase greatly, but it will also be reciprocated.

The staff and temporary faculty marching through the research university define their problems in more industrial, job-related or union terms than do the ladder faculty members. To the extent that the ladder faculty members incorporate this support staff into the larger intellectual enterprise as important contributors, the more harmonious and more productive the institution will become.

---

* F. M. Cornford, *Microcosmographia Academica*, Cambridge, Bowes and Bowes (1908), Appendix (p189).

Chapter 7

Governing Boards

*The responsibilities of a trustee can be
onerous. A trustee carries the fiduciary
responsibility and liability to use the trust
assets according to the provisions of the
trust instrument.*

— Internet definition

A successful board of trustees or regents, who have final
authority over the university, consists of productive and
experienced citizen-counselors from many professions including ex officio university officers who bring skills and viewpoints
that challenge and broaden the institution. Trustees keep the
university aware of larger societal developments and demands
as they impinge on the academy. But trustees also learn about
the university, why it has the programs and plans it does, and
in turn they can explain or sell the university to the larger community. In addition to this communicative role, the board has
final authority over university finances and programs. Board
influence, when properly applied, is not exerted directly on the
university, but through its chief executive officer, the president.
Presidents and their staffs in turn are responsible for implementing regental policies within available funds.

Unless you are the chief campus officer or act in that role
on occasion, your interaction with trustees will be casual and
remote. If board meetings are open, you can be sure that critical issues will always be deferred to executive sessions. Trustees

are observed at ceremonial events such as graduation, and are heard primarily through their written word in local publications. If their administrative team is effective, trustees limit themselves to policy and financial issues and do not micromanage the institution. Their actions might include land acquisition or sales, funding of capital improvements in competition with faculty and staff salaries, approval of architectural firms, approval of fundraising goals, questioning whether the student health service should provide gay counseling and abortions (controversial political issues don't occur only in legislatures), formulating investment strategies for the endowment, determining the availability of endowment funds to support programs in the institution, reviewing benefits packages for faculty and staff, review of hiring effectiveness in relation to salaries, reviewing recruitment of athletes and the salaries of coaches, approval of the president's budget or, in state universities, formulation of strategies for presenting a budget to the legislature and the governor, review of lawsuits against the university, review of sexual harassment policies and disciplinary protocols, review of administrative salaries and benefit packages, appearance at ceremonial events, lectures, and athletic events, and dealing with one-issue groups.

The institutional mission statement must be constantly reviewed and updated so that new trustees will internalize the objectives of the institution. Assuming there is agreement on the mission of the institution, trustees must ask whether the mission is being followed. We know that all institutions need more money, but what is the institution doing with its present resources? Does it really need more money, or does it need better management? If it needs better management, is the present president the one who can provide it, or should that person be replaced? It has been said that the first action at any board meeting should be to ask, "Should we fire the president?" If the answer is no, boards should then spend their time working on how to support their chief executives and their institutional programs. The president is the board's most important appointment as well as its most important sacrifice when the president's political bank account, energy, or ability is exhausted.

Usually the board delegates a portion of its authority to various officers and faculty committees within the institution. As examples, day-to-day operation of the university is delegated to the president and his staff. The content of courses, requirements for degrees, and evaluations of program academic quality are usually delegated to the faculty who also recommend students to the board for granting of degrees. As illustrated later in this chapter, if the board loses faith in the integrity of the administrative or faculty processes, what is granted can also be taken away. In the best of all worlds, trustees have a deep understanding of the goals or mission of the institution, its processes, and its frailties. They become informed, and resist the terrible urge to micromanage the institution directly rather than work through their chief executive officer, the president.

Regents at the University of Colorado

The University of Colorado, where I served as interim chancellor of the Boulder campus for two and one half years, has nine elected regents who serve six-year terms. There is one regent for each congressional district, and two who are elected at large. While many of my interactions with the regents were benign and productive, there were also rough spots.

Before my first regents' meeting in 1994 I learned that the board intended to deny a merit increase to a professor of English because in a book on Greek myths and art, which he had submitted in support of this merit increase, he had published a photograph of a Greek vase that portrayed sexual activities that certain regents found pornographic. Though I did my best to point out during the meeting that regental denial of this merit increase had all the elements of denial of free speech and academic freedom, the regents proceeded to deny the pay raise. Within hours the *Chronicle of Higher Education* was on the telephone, prepared to write a story about the regents' action. Fortunately the regents reversed themselves before their next meeting and the matter settled down.

A second event of this sort occurred when I checked with various members of the board to make certain I had their support for a student-housing bond issue that appeared on their agenda later in the week. After having received their assurances—"Yes Rod, we are with you"—I walked into the board meeting only to have a critical vote by one member reversed. He voted against the bond issue with no warning to me. His switch reminded me of a statement on the "deal" in politics often attributed to Jesse Unruh, for many years a powerful politician in California: "You always have to hold back ten percent for the double-cross!" I also received telephone calls from certain regents complaining about the grades of a supporter's child. "My neighbor's child received a C+ in a course when she should have received a B−." Would I please look into this and report back? Perhaps their elective method of selection is why some CU regents behaved on occasion more like politicians running for office than a deliberative board.

New trustees or regents may be selected in a variety of ways: by the incumbents themselves on a self-perpetuating board, as is the case in some private institutions (The Harvard Corporation); they may be elected by the general population or alumni, as is the case with public school boards and a few state universities (Michigan and Colorado); or they may be appointed by the state governor with legislative approval (California). Some universities, such as the University of Vermont, are governed by a combination of elected and appointed regents, and many have ex officio representation by state officials and presidents of alumni, student, or faculty associations. The method of selection, being a human process, is not the linchpin that produces an effective board. All these selection processes work if the wisest and most experienced people assume trustee positions.

Many trustees are themselves managers of large, hierarchical institutions, often businesses, which, compared to the decentralized and somewhat feudal nature of the university, are highly streamlined. An efficient, flexible, for-profit corporation can rapidly change directions to respond to changing markets, can eliminate workers and staff, and can measure its performance by the efficiency with which it produces a quality product in relation to its competitors. University board members, while having responsibilities similar to those of their counterparts on business boards, must deal with circumstances that are absent in the business world. That an excess of tenured faculty in the foreign languages, for example, is restricting hiring in the rapidly expanding field of computer science seems a simple problem to a trustee who has not encountered the traditions, symbolism, and legal constraints of faculty tenure. That there is a tradition of "shared governance" in which the administration, though it has the authority to act, is obliged to consult with faculty and student committees before acting seems impossibly cumbersome to trustees from the outer world beyond the university. Still it is possible to deal with these obstructions if one knows which levers to pull!

Before I went to the University of Colorado, I always believed that the academic quality of an institution was immediately related to the quality of its board of trustees and key members of the administration. The faculty at Boulder disproved that hypothesis! The academic quality of the Boulder faculty exceeded considerably the quality of the University of Colorado administration, which has been for a rather tumultuous administrative ride over the past twenty years. Perhaps the fact that the administrative parade is so much shorter than that of the faculty is responsible for this unexpected paradox.

When Boards Lose Confidence in an Institution's Ability to Govern Itself

At the Berkeley campus of the University of California in fall 1968, four faculty members in charge of an experimental course, Social Analysis 139X, "Dehumanization and Regeneration in American Social Order," decided to hire activist Eldridge Cleaver as a guest instructor to give ten lectures in the course. The actual organizers of the course were part of the Center for Participant Education, a non-faculty, self-appointed group who found faculty sponsors for various nontraditional course proposals, and brokered their implementation between the faculty and the Board of Educational Development (BED). The BED was the official campus administrative structure for sponsoring such nontraditional courses, having been set up for this purpose in response to a recommendation from the Muscatine committee who wrote *Education at Berkeley.*

Eldridge Cleaver in 1968 was known as the author of *Soul on Ice,* a best-selling book; as the Black Panther Party Minister of Information; as The Peace and Freedom Party presidential candidate for the fall 1968 US presidential election; and as a felon on parole. Further, Cleaver was awaiting trial following a shootout with Oakland police in which over 1,000 shots were fired and a policeman and a Black Panther were killed. The trial was scheduled to commence shortly after he would finish his lectures in Social Analysis 139X.

On Tuesday, September 17, 1968, the California State Senate, having been alerted that the regents would discuss this appointment at their September meeting, debated this action and voted 33-2 to censure university administrators University President Charles Hitch (Clark Kerr had been fired twenty months earlier), and Berkeley Chancellor Roger Heyns for the Cleaver appointment. On the following Thursday, the same day as the monthly regents' meeting in Los Angeles, the State Assembly, despite the efforts of Assembly Speaker Jesse Unruh, joined the Senate and added the Board of Regents to the censure list by a vote of 41-22. Within hours the Senate also adopted this addition. Governor Ronald Reagan, an ex officio regent of the university, had set the stage for a showdown—or shootout—on who runs the university, at the regents' meeting scheduled for later that week. Since 1920, the Board of Regents had delegated total responsibility for the conduct of courses to the faculty. Now it appeared that the regents were about to remove this authority and make such determinations on their own. Their resolve was undoubtedly reinforced by Governor Reagan's two most recent appointments to the board, an advertising executive from Los Angeles, H. R. Haldeman (of subsequent Watergate fame), and W. Glenn Campbell, director of the Hoover Institution at Stanford.

This imminent local institutional crisis blossomed in a larger arena of national malaise. In the previous six months both Martin Luther King and Robert Kennedy had been assassinated. There had been extensive violence between demonstrators and police at the Democratic convention in Chicago only three weeks before. The Vietnam War was continuing to sap American self-confidence and to polarize the young against the old. As the 1968 September regents' meeting opened, compromise was not on the minds of many.

On the first day of their meeting, Thursday, Sept. 19, 1968, the Regents' Educational Policy Committee, following a four-hour debate, decided to throw the entire issue to the full Board of Regents, which met the next day. A regental vote to ban Social Analysis 139X, a move sought by Regent Reagan and his supporters, would de facto remove from the faculty final approval of courses, a right they had exercised for almost fifty years. That same day, Santa Clara University, a Catholic institution, announced that it had invited Cleaver to lecture, an invitation that was soon also extended by Stanford University, UC Davis,

UC Riverside, UCLA, and Sacramento State College, among others. President Hitch searched desperately for a compromise to avoid a confrontation on academic freedom that would most certainly lead to censure by the American Association of University Professors. Academic censure produces a similar effect to censure by the National Collegiate Athletic Association. When the NCAA imposes penalties on an institution, it becomes much more difficult to attract quality athletes to that institution. So it is with attracting faculty members, who are reluctant to commit their careers to an institution that shows overt disregard for academic freedom.

President Hitch knew that Harvard University policy allowed only one lecture per course offering by guest lecturers. In his compromise proposal he suggested that the University of California policy should be a maximum of two presentations by a guest lecturer. The regents rejected this proposal, but accepted by a vote of 10-8 the Harvard policy that would allow Cleaver one lecture instead of ten. The chairman of the Berkeley Division of the Academic Senate, Robert Powell, a chemist, was to determine whether the restructured course deserved academic credit, and was to report the result to the "Regents, the President and the Chancellor of the Berkeley campus." Regent Philip Boyd authored the censure resolution, which was passed without dissent, concluding, "The Regents consider that in this instance the trust that follows such delegation to the Academic Senate has been abused; therefore the regents censure those within the Berkeley Division of the Academic Senate and the Board of Educational Development who were responsible."*

Three additional regents' decisions at the same meeting set other restrictions on campus activity. Most alarming to the faculty was resolution 4, which stated, "While recognizing the primacy of the Academic Senate in approving courses and

---

* *The Daily Californian,* Sept. 20, 1968.

curricula, the Regents direct the President to initiate an exploration with the Academic Senate of the appropriate role of the administration in this area of joint concern." The possible loss of delegated responsibility for conduct of courses confirmed the faculty's worst fears.

The regents also challenged the First Amendment, instructing the chancellors of each campus to "take whatever steps may be necessary to assure that future campus dramatic productions conform to accepted standards of good taste and do not portray lewd, indecent, or obscene conduct." In addition, they ordered the Academic Senate to formulate a set of explicit academic standards for the planning, staffing, conduct, and evaluation of experimental courses, to be submitted to the regents at their January 1969 meeting. State Superintendent of Public Instruction Max Rafferty, who was an ex officio regent as well as a Republican senatorial candidate, said after the meeting that he was surprised the regents were spending so much time on the issue. He said that Cleaver was "a graduate of San Quentin High and as qualified to teach as I am to be head surgeon at the Mayo Clinic."* Campus response was immediate and predictable.

On October 3, 1968, the day after the first meeting of Social Analysis 139X, the Academic Freedom Committee of the Berkeley Division, chaired by philosopher John Searle, announced "The Berkeley Division of the Senate declares that the regents' hasty and ill-considered action was a violation of the academic freedom and autonomy of the Senate, of the Board of Educational Development and of the faculty responsible for course 139X." The Academic Freedom Committee further encouraged those responsible to carry on the program of instruction and urged the BED to take all appropriate steps necessary to issue credit for the course. That same day Eldridge Cleaver entered the debate himself, announcing to the students at a noon rally

---

* *The Daily Californian,* Sept. 24, 1968.

in Sproul Plaza that if the regents closed the door on 139X, "you have no recourse than to take to the street."

The regents were adamant and not about to move as indicated by Governor Reagan's comment the next day, "Those of you who are unwilling to teach or unwilling to learn within our educational framework can damn well get your education somewhere else."*

Before the next regents' meeting on October 13, the students announced a takeover of the university unless the regents retreated from their stand. The students then stormed the regents' meeting at Santa Cruz the next day. The regents did not retreat, but, on President Hitch's urging, did, by a vote of 13-8, reject Regent Ronald Reagan's request to strip the faculty of most of its powers. Reagan's motion had stated, among other things, "any faculty member who, by any form of stratagem or subterfuge accredits work in Social Analysis 139X would be subject to disciplinary action" and the credit would not count toward graduation.

The following week the students organized two sit-ins at Berkeley and demanded that credit be given to 139X. At the first sit-in, in Sproul Hall on October 22, 120 students were arrested. The second occurred the next day in the office of the Dean of the College of Letters and Science, in Moses Hall. The protesters barricaded themselves in the dean's office until the next morning, when police broke in and removed them. Chancellor Heyns recommended suspension or dismissal for all the students who were arrested.

Meanwhile Social Analysis 139X had been meeting regularly, though the question of academic credit was held in abeyance. Students reported that Eldridge Cleaver appeared to have covered most of his material after three or four lectures and was devoting increased amounts of lecture time to

---

* *The Daily Californian,* Oct. 4, 1968.

question-and-answer sessions. Later on the day of the Moses Hall sit-in arrests, Cleaver gave his 139X lecture, saying nothing about the sit-in whose object had been to obtain credit for the course.

During the question period an earnest young woman sitting in the front of class asked, "Mr. Cleaver, last night a large number of us sat in at the dean's office in Moses Hall to obtain credit for this course, and we were arrested. You have said nothing about our actions. Where do you stand on that?" Per students in the class Cleaver is reported to have replied, "We don't need you guilt-ridden, white, middle-class youth. You weren't with us yesterday, and you won't be with us tomorrow! We don't need you."

Two events brought the immediate crisis of regental intervention in a faculty-sponsored course to a close. First was that the regents, at their November 22 meeting, authorized the president to make exceptions to the one-lecture policy for guest instructors. At the same time, they refused to grant credit for course 139X. The following week, on November 27, just before the Thanksgiving recess, the Berkeley faculty, by a vote of 278-143, authorized the Committee on Courses to reorganize 139X for five units of credit.

Though the immediate crisis had passed, the mutual distrust between the regents and the faculty would persist for many years, until enough new marchers had entered both groups to dim their collective memories.

November 27, 1968 was the same day that S. I. "Sleepy Sam" Hayakawa became the president of San Francisco State College. That campus was headed for a period of violence greater than anything seen at Berkeley. Both the Kent State shootings and the Third World Strike at Berkeley would occur later that academic year. During the Third World Strike, the California National Guard would occupy the Berkeley campus, and Governor Ronald Reagan would accomplish what no student strike had ever done—he would close the campus. Those of us who lived through the crises of 1968 and 1969 still remember them clearly, even though the events took place forty years ago. Twenty years from now these events will only be recalled from history. May future university marchers never have to relive them!

Will history repeat itself? Will the confrontations of the 1960s reoccur in universities? University administrators, like parents, can never anticipate all the passions that may inflame future students. But more safety valves now exist for communication, and students, whether we like it or not, have assumed many adult roles—including the right to vote—that were denied them in the early 1960s. Perhaps any bad plays in the future will feature new scripts and will not be reruns of old ones.

As a new academic administrator you now have in hand a guidebook to the tribal groups with whom you will negotiate, persuade, and, if successful, will lead. What follows in this short tutorial are some accounts of how this process works. There are no absolute answers here, but some examples of how and how not to be effective!

Chapter 8

It's Only the Janitor!

What Impelled Me to Recount Some "On-the-Job-Training" Experiences

Spring 1986 at the Berkeley campus brought our traditional political pageant. This Berkeley phenomenon can be compared with a Christmas pageant except that, rather than celebrating a birth, it celebrates the awakening of the adolescent political spirit. The participants' motivations range from sincere interest in large-scale moral problems, which we often face for the first time at college, to cynical use of any issue at hand as a match to start the prairie fire of revolution.

The difference in 1986 was that the issue, divestment from firms doing business in South Africa, was not new. In 1972 students at Harvard University (possibly because, on average, they came from more sophisticated financial backgrounds than did their Berkeley counterparts) had begun to protest the Harvard Corporation's investment policies. The protesters maintained that the corporation's stock-investment decisions did not take into account whether the activities of their portfolio firms doing business in South Africa were furthering apartheid. They subsequently extended their protest to a broader range of investor social-responsibility issues by investigating how the Harvard Corporation voted proxies on its stock on matters ranging from manufacture of nuclear weapons to the sale of milk formula for African babies. How Harvard voted its stock, to the surprise of those protesting, was not the numerical lever that would alter corporate direction. Harvard's equity ownership, compared with total stock outstanding in any given firm, was very small. Instead, Harvard's position on proxy issues was primarily of symbolic and political importance, a fact not lost on the protesters.

Fourteen years later, Berkeley students awoke to the fact that the regents of the University of California, because they administer their own retirement system, invest sums much greater than those controlled by the Harvard Corporation. The University of California, like Harvard, is a good theater for press coverage on controversial issues, and the symbolism of the issue fit well with Berkeley symbolic politics. The protesters' strategy at Berkeley was to bring attention to the divestment issue, using civil disobedience if necessary, through actions on Sproul Plaza, cradle of the Free Speech Movement of the '60s, and in front of California Hall, the Berkeley administration building. Though the administration at Berkeley had no control over the regents' investment policy, it was, and remains, the local symbol of university authority, and is always an adequate target for protesters' actions.

A challenge to campus administrations is to ensure two rights that are not always compatible: the right to protest and the right to study and learn without disruption. The resolution of these goals, when conflict exists, will always tread the gray zone of acceptable student conduct, and successful protesters will always have chalk on their shoes from playing close to the foul line.

No exception, the 1986 apartheid protest moved beyond the usual noon rally. A new protest strategy emerged, erecting and occupying plywood and cardboard shanties in a politically prominent place. Nearly every free backyard within a mile of campus became a site for prefabrication of a shanty to be assembled at a predetermined time on some symbolic site. At the designated hour, protesting groups began to march from all corners of the campus to erect their huts in front of California Hall. They wanted to make a strong political statement that would, and did, receive extensive press coverage. The action was also potentially within the limits of campus rules as long as the shanties did not interfere with ongoing campus activities or constitute a safety hazard. This multi-front invasion confounded the small number of campus police on duty. Shanty building started in mid-afternoon on April 2, 1986. After three hours of incessant hammering and shouting by several hundred protesters, some forty shanties had appeared. Fortunately for the administration, the shanties blocked the entrance to California Hall and were declared a fire hazard by the fire marshal, giving the university a reason for removing them.

The first rule of protester removal from university facilities is act fast.

The occupation is either ended within twenty-four hours, or one is in for a protracted standoff involving regents, the ACLU, court orders, politicians, the press, faculty, students, and parents. The occupation of shanties placed in open spaces in Harvard Yard that same spring was not ended quickly. It extended through graduation, much to the distress of many Harvard alumni and the Harvard administration. That administration had not followed this first rule, but to its credit, bit the bullet in favor of the First Amendment, and, under vocal alumni criticism, left the shanties in place until their occupants became bored or exhausted.

On the basis of the Berkeley fire marshal's order, the decision was made to remove the shanties, and the protesters were warned to move them or face arrest. Acceptance of this warning would have meant submission to university demands and the failure of civil disobedience. It was duly rejected. In retrospect, the principal failing of the administration was insufficient regard for the second rule of protester occupation, which is:

If you are going to remove protesters peaceably, do it with overwhelming numbers of enforcers (usually the police).

An attempt to end civil disobedience with an insufficient number of police almost always results in unnecessary violence.

By midnight, the campus police had obtained aid from other campuses of the university and from surrounding police departments, but not from the city of Berkeley, whose police department was under orders from the left-wing Berkeley City Council not to cooperate. The campus police chief announced that the protesters must leave or face arrest for trespassing. This pronouncement merely activated the Berkeley telephone tree and brought out still more protesters. By the time the arrests started, shortly after midnight on April 3, the beginnings of a riot were under way. A bottle- and rock-throwing crowd was taunting the police lines. Violence increased, and the crowd began to hurl whatever it could find through the windows of California Hall, the administration building. The second rule of crowd control had not been followed. There were insufficient police both to hold the lines and to make the arrests. Finally, at about 2:00 a.m., a halt was called to the arrests until more police could be secured through mutual aid. The Oakland motorcycle force, an intimidating group, was summoned, but would not arrive in Berkeley until almost dawn.

As the chief administrative representative on the scene, I had come prepared for a long, cold night, arriving about 8:00 p.m. in my sailing clothes and a watch cap. From inside the police lines I watched the whole sordid affair unfold. I finally determined at about 5:00 a.m. to call university president David Gardner, knowing that he would soon be called by reporters and that he hated surprises. The police slipped me into California Hall through a side door. Amid the broken glass, I found a telephone and informed President Gardner about our sorry predicament. He received the information in his matter-of-fact style and told me to keep him informed.

How was I to get out of the building? The three policemen inside California Hall decided the safest way would be to go out the front door right behind the slogan-covered plywood shanties. The arrests had recommenced under the glare of xenon lamps, which gave the front of California Hall the appearance of a stage set within a proscenium arch. The front doors of the hall are much taller than the shanties, and could be seen from all corners of the area in front and from across the police lines. When one of these doors was opened about six inches to let me escape, a cry went up outside: "They're coming through the back, they're coming through the back." I emerged through the plywood shanties in my sailing jacket and watch cap, and a new cry went up: "It's only the janitor, it's only the janitor." Unknowingly, the crowd had just characterized much of my job! Cleaning up administrative disarray had become a significant part of my efforts, possibly because of my endurance rather than my skill. It is ironic that the crowd that night, a bastion of Berkeley political correctness, should use the term "only the janitor." For years now the term "custodian" has been preferred by those who carry the title "janitor." The modifier "only" speaks for itself.

As I walked through the broken shanties, torn cardboard, and a motley crowd of shouting people, dawn was bringing ugly reality to what, a few hours earlier, had been an illuminated stage set. I mused, "Why have I come to see this bad play again? I thought I taught this course last year!"

Perhaps something could be learned from such experiences. I would try writing them down.

Chapter 9

Lesson 1 – Learn from Mistakes

The passage of time has tempered my thoughts on two administrative fiascoes of which I was a part. In the first, forty years ago, I was an observer. In the second, twenty years ago, I was a participant. Though the emotion has subsided, the memory of these events is still vivid, and my recollections of them, though the view of only one person, may provide some insights for readers about to venture into the world of academic administration and politics.

As an Observer: The 1960s Student Rebellion

What country ever existed a century and a half without a rebellion? ... The tree of liberty must be refreshed from time to time with the blood of patriots and tyrants. It is the natural manure.

— Thomas Jefferson, 1787

This first fiasco occurred in fall 1964 during the FSM, which marked a rebirth of student activism at CAL. The issue, in its initial stage, was the right of students to participate in political advocacy on campus. Political neutrality on campus had always been regental and campus policy, probably to gain ecumenical political support. But a new awareness of the oppression of Black citizens in the United States had mobilized the passions of many students, and they were prepared to speak out against this injustice on campus no matter what the administration believed was a wise policy. The escalation of the issue centered on the right of the students to set up card tables in Sproul Plaza as centers of advocacy for various causes. The administration, by its own predilection, and under pressure from regents and many legislators, maintained the old policy against political advocacy on campus. In fall 1964, there were a series of escalations and confrontations over this policy, culminating in several thousand students surrounding a campus police car on Sproul Plaza in which Jack Weinberg was being held in custody. Students held the police car captive for twenty hours. By then the situation was fairly well out of hand, and the local campus administration had become, in the eyes of the regents at least, neutralized and ineffective as they lost control.

After the police car incident, protest rallies on Sproul Plaza escalated so that soon 5,000–10,000 people came to Sproul Plaza each noon hour to listen to the latest developments in the contest over student's rights to exercise political advocacy on the Berkeley campus. I soon noticed that these rallies shared much with a tent revival meeting. First the air was filled with the sense of impending change and improvement. The forces of evil would be overcome, and those organizing the event knew how to do it. There was a strong sense that morality and righteousness would overcome oppression, and there was security in the large numbers attending the rally who believed likewise. The agendas were similarly organized. The rally might start with music and singing; there were warm-up speakers, a calendar of events, passing of the hat, and finally the major event—the equivalent of a sermon—an inspiring speech on the issues that served as a certification of what participants sensed was a revolutionary undertaking. There was cheering and applause during the speech, and, on occasion, the audience response reached the participatory level of a revival meeting.

But most poignant of all was what sometimes followed. At one rally, Mario Savio proclaimed that the workings of the machine (the university) had become so oppressive and so odious that it could be allowed to go on no longer. It must be stopped, and the oppressed must throw themselves on the gears and wheels to bring the insensible machine down. The collective effect of his speech was electric, and when Mr. Savio suggested that the students march into Sproul Hall behind him for a passive sit-in to indicate their anger and dismay, there was overwhelming response. Joan Baez, who was a young folk singer at that time and a strong supporter of the movement, chose to sing "The Lord's Prayer" as the crowd, mostly students, marched through the doors of Sproul Hall. This remarkable scene was the revival-tent call to come forward, walk the sawdust path, and be saved. Guilt-ridden, mostly white, middle-class youth, who for the most part had never experienced formal religion, climbed the steps of Sproul Hall to engage in civil disobedience and redemption. During one of these rallies, a colleague of mine in the Botany Department, whose father was a Presbyterian minister, said, while we both stood under his umbrella, "The problem with this group is that they never went to Sunday school. They never read the Old Testament. They don't understand retribution!"

I recount these emotions underlying the FSM rallies only to indicate a reality that was not understood by the administration and President Clark Kerr when he called his fateful meeting of December 7, 1964, in the Greek Theatre. Backed by a council of eighty department chairs commanded to attend, and other university officials, President Kerr hoped to reassert the role of the university administration and to convince the campus community to side with him to restore calm and order on the Berkeley campus—or at least that was his intent. What Kerr and his administrative colleagues failed to internalize was the political and emotional intensity of the rallies being held in Sproul Plaza.

The Greek Theatre, site of speeches by world leaders from President Teddy Roosevelt to Adlai Stevenson and Corazon Aquino, had in recent years become better known as the site of Bill Graham's rock concerts. The "Greek" is a 10,000-seat open amphitheater situated just where the Berkeley campus begins to ascend into the Berkeley Hills. When large crowds are present, as they were that day, the floor is also filled with temporary seating. I sat there with my departmental colleagues to hear our president resolve the conflicts that were wracking our university. The theater was filled to overflowing. The department chairs, headed by Political Science Department chair Robert Scalapino, sat behind President Kerr on the raised stage. Many of the chairs sympathized with the students and had been reluctant to join the group, but succumbed to administrative pressure. Obviously, what was to become a motto for the movement, "Question Authority," was not operative to the extent that it is today. By today's standards the audience was remarkably polite.

Kerr began his speech. After several sentences it was evident to me that he was off the mark, and when he said in his opening comments that the Greek Theatre "has seen great operatic and theatrical performances," he didn't realize that he and his staff were just about to produce the most unusual theater that most of us would ever experience. The audience had come to hear about the issues from a human being with "egg on his tie." That is not what they got. President Kerr, in his controlled businesslike way, informed the audience that the regents had approved a policy authorizing "on-campus political activity for lawful purposes," but that the legal details had to be worked out. He spoke of the need to restore order if the university was to retain political support. The speech, like President Kerr himself, was not passionate.[*] His statement of the university's devotion to the First and Fourteenth Amendments to the Constitution were just not believed by many of those present. His call for unity, if we were to march forward to the greater glory of the university, sounded to many of us as if it had been prepared for a graduation ceremony at a small liberal arts college. The crowd, unlike the audiences of today under similar circumstances, was quiet.

When the speech was finished, Robert Scalapino, the chair of the council that had joined President Kerr onstage, announced, "The meeting is adjourned." As he was saying this, Mario Savio appeared, striding out from the left side of the stage to address the audience. The crowd was frozen with anticipation. Scalapino said again, "This meeting is over." By this time Savio was halfway to the podium. Suddenly three policemen appeared from the back of the stage, grabbed Savio by his arm and necktie, and dragged him to the rear in front of 10,000 witnesses. The audience was stunned. The student leader of the FSM had been denied free speech by force. After momentary disbelief, the crowd surged forward toward the stage, roaring their dismay and disapproval. Imagining that if this were South America, 200 people were about to be killed in a riot, I said to the senior professor on my right, Leonard Machlis, "What do you think is safe?" He said, "Let's stay right here"—a wise choice under the circumstances. When the stage was cleared and Kerr and the department chairs had departed, Savio, now liberated, again walked out onstage. To great cheers from the assembled, and without microphone, he invited them all to a rally on Sproul

---

[*] Online archive of the University of California, Release 11 am December 7, 1964.

Plaza to commence immediately, a rally where he said, "there is true free speech."

What had started as an administrative attempt to recover a sticky situation had done exactly the opposite. I never expect to see such a fiasco in front of so many people again. Why did the administration fail so ignominiously? I believe they were too distant from the politically motivated students and from changes in political attitudes among the young. Even if they had been able to read Charles Reich's *The Greening of America* in 1962, eight years before its publication, they would not have believed any part of it and would probably have made the same mistakes. "Power to the People" and "One Man, One Vote" were slogans that symbolized the views of the more radical constituencies, who believed that a commune should govern the Berkeley campus and the administration should be relegated to keeping chalk at the blackboards and the lawns mowed. The radicals posed a threat to administrators, who had not previously dealt with similar challenges. The administrators could have declared that a successful university must always be sensitive to the needs and desires of students; that in the final analysis educational decisions will be made by the faculty; and that in this sense, education is not a democratic process. But they resisted any discussion, although this policy is what emerged at Berkeley over the next forty years. Decision making at Berkeley during Chancellor Heyman's years became more open and inclusive, while the administration and faculty retained final authority in decision making. The Berkeley administration in 1964 apparently did not understand that they could extend their consultation on campus issues much more widely without diminishing their authority or responsibility to govern.

Faculty members who were at Berkeley during the 1960s differ about the consequences of the student movement and whether a more perceptive administration could have changed its course. Many of us who attended the rallies sensed there was a pent-up dam of angry energy that had to run its course and that could not be neutralized by negotiation with the administration. Others believed then and now that history is not inevitable, and that its course is subject to man's rational intervention. The truth, as with most such matters, lies somewhere in between. If Clark Kerr's meeting had been a success, if it had offered a process for resolving not only the issue of free speech, but also the more fundamental issue of who runs the university, the path of the student movement that finally led to the violence of the Third World Strike in 1969 might have been shortened. But these issues were a political reality that only negotiation, accommodation, and the passage of time could soothe.

In retrospect, it is ironic that the political punch aimed at the university produced only moderate and, most of us believe, beneficial change in the university itself. None of us anticipated in the 1960s that the institution that would be radically changed as an aftermath to the student movement was not the university, but rather the city of Berkeley. A radical punch had been launched at the university. The university ducked. The city received the blow.

A number of the UC students during the 1960s and early '70s continued to live in Berkeley, and transferred their vision for the world to what was most accessible to them, Berkeley politics and political correctness. But by the Berkeley elections of the early 1990s, there was some retreat from the political fallout of the student movement. Not only were current UC undergraduates not born when the '60s wave of radicalism swept the campus, some of their parents were not born either. The student parade marches on, each generation having to relearn the lessons of its predecessors. Many of the faculty members who were at Berkeley in the '60s have departed. Undoubtedly at some future time the students, faculty, and administration at Berkeley will once again address the issues of the FSM, namely the balancing of individual freedom with the mission and prerogatives of the institution. Their answers will be rediscovered in the context of that time, one hopes with continued love and respect for a remarkable place.

As a Participant: Race-Based Admissions

When an institution is far from its affirmative action goals, the job to be done is evident, and the policies to achieve goals are not under great scrutiny, but as the goals are approached, there will be a legitimate demand for careful balancing of interests among competing groups. In my experience, it will be impossible to retain the confidence of these groups without being public about policy, process and result.

— RBP 1989

The student movement at Berkeley in the 1960s and early '70s was in part about access to the university by people often denied access by either historical accident or design. Nonetheless, during this same period, possible racial discrimination in freshman admissions to Berkeley was not an issue. We were not overenrolled. We were receiving just enough eligible applications from high school seniors to maintain our undergraduate student population as we admitted every eligible freshman applicant. From the standpoint of easing enrollment pressures, the student unrest at Berkeley during the '60s had been a boon. Many parents and other counselors were reluctant to recommend Berkeley to high school seniors because they perceived the Berkeley campus as politically, socially, and intellectually risky. Their concern caused increased enrollment pressure on other UC campuses farther from the realities of urban issues, such as Santa Cruz and Davis. Under these circumstances the issue of freshman access at Berkeley would not arise, as no group of citizens could claim they were being denied access to Berkeley in favor of someone else. This blissful state of affairs existed until 1974 when the Berkeley policy of accepting all eligible applicants would have yielded more registrations than available spaces.

In an oversubscribed public university, the question of which student applicants are admitted is a contentious public policy debate among the applicants and their parents, the legislature, the voters, the faculty, the trustees, and the administration. In the academic year 2005, 36,982 high school seniors applied to Berkeley; 8,777 were admitted, and 4,101 enrolled. The question is, and will always be, in the minds of those 28,205 who were not admitted, was the selection process "fair"?

The adolescent years in high school are a time of growth and blossoming for the potentials of every student. For the most part, students do not have to gain competitive admission to their local high school, and thus attendance at a publicly supported institution such as Berkeley is seen as a right, not a privilege. For many students, application to college is their first brush with the fact that opportunity may not be unlimited and that they may be rejected from a desired career pathway. This experience is not only traumatic for students; it can be even more traumatic for parents, who feel responsible for assuring the success of their offspring. It is natural that a denial of admission should be questioned. It turns out that the word "fair" has become useless in this debate. Like the group called Asian-Americans for Fair Admissions, corresponding groups have been formed for almost every other ethnic and behavioral group. With many definitions of what is "fair," it became more useful to think about what makes sound public policy and balances the academic distinction of the University of California with the political realities of the state and its needs, not about ten or twenty conflicting definitions of the word "fair."

I first encountered the strident politics of this issue at a meeting of the University of California regents in November 1987. It was, in retrospect, a case study both of how large organizations lose the confidence of their publics and of how they painstakingly rebuild it. Recent events at other universities have shown us that public confidence may be lost in many ways, in the wake of athletic scandals or the inclusion of questionable charges in the calculation of overhead rates on grants and contracts, but the perceived fairness of undergraduate admissions to a public university strikes closer to home for many citizens than any other issue.

Most of the work at a monthly University of California regents' meeting is done on the first of two days, when regental committees meet and prepare their recommendations for approval by the entire board on the second day. The second day generally opens with the president's report on news of the university, followed by a topical report from one of the campuses on an issue of interest or concern to the regents. The issue scheduled for November 1987 was a review of the undergraduate admissions process at Berkeley, in response to concerns of the Asian community. Alleged illegal discrimination against Asian applicants for freshman admission had been documented in The Asian-American Task Force Report. This report was followed by an investigation by the auditor general of California, the results of which were published as *A Review of First-Year Admission of Asians and Caucasians at the University of California at Berkeley*, in October 1987, just before the November regents' meeting. The Berkeley campus had responded to its findings with a report proclaiming that the auditor general had misinterpreted the data and that the university had been and remained innocent.

At that time, Berkeley, like all UC campuses, admitted 94 percent of its freshmen from only the top one eighth (or 12.5 percent) of California high school graduates, as measured by grades in required courses and test scores. (About 6 percent of admissions were reserved for special action, students with special talents and promise who were not technically eligible.)

In the College of Letters and Science the eligible (top 12.5 percent) high school graduates were admitted in three tiers. The first tier, 40 percent, was admitted on the basis of the highest grades and test scores alone. The second tier was admitted on grades and test scores plus seven "supplementary criteria," with a total of 1,300 points that could be added to the algorithm of grades plus test scores. Six of the supplementary criteria were totally objective: Was the applicant from a rural high school? Did the applicant have special talents or hardship? Was the applicant a California resident? The seventh criterion was an essay that counted for 500 of the 1,300 possible supplementary points. The third tier consisted of eligible high school graduates who brought special talents and diversity to the class—underrepresented minorities, rural residents, handicapped people, and those with unusual musical or athletic talents.

A sequence of events ignited the Asian American concerns. Starting in the early 1980s, the Berkeley campus, in order to increase the enrollment of underrepresented minorities, started assuring all eligible (those in the top 12.5 percent of California high school graduates) Black, Chicano, and Native American high school seniors that they would be automatically admitted to Berkeley. Was a policy of increasing underrepresented minority enrollment appropriate for a state-funded university?

We believed it was.* That we were under-enrolled for freshman admission made our task easy, as all eligible students were admitted, and since no one was denied admission, no one could claim discrimination. We should have realized that the number of eligible applicants of all races would skyrocket in future years, but we did not. We should have foreseen the freshman admissions controversy both earlier and more clearly.

The trend toward increased eligible applications continued throughout the remainder of the 1970s, though as recently as 1980 Berkeley still accepted two-thirds of its eligible applicants for freshman admission. But by 1984, the number of freshman applicants increased from 9,006 to 12,381 (or 37 percent). When, in 1986, the University of California allowed freshman applicants to apply to more than one campus, the total number of applicants to Berkeley jumped to 20,291, and it reached 22,439 in 1988. In fourteen years the number of high school seniors applying to Berkeley had jumped from 4,706 to 22,439, or 477 percent. Another development exacerbated the enrollment

---

* Prestigious private universities, who also believed in diversifying their undergraduate student bodies, had an easier time implementing changes. Derek Bok, who was president during my term as a Harvard overseer, once observed at one of our overseers' meetings that a major challenge for a Harvard president between overseer meetings was "to find a task to keep the overseers busy" and presumably out of areas that could prove inconvenient for the Harvard administration. Bok had a unique talent for doing this. After the first full day of overseer committee meetings, he would sit by a floor lamp in the president's house, legs crossed, gazing down at a yellow legal pad, and drone on endlessly without pause about the state of the campus. Soon his audience began to long for dinner and a cocktail beforehand. As a result there were few questions from this elected group of alumni that might cause disquiet in the Harvard Yard. At one session there was a question: "Just what is Harvard doing about diversifying the undergraduate student body?" The answer was a stunner. "Every year in the United States there are only 700 Afro-American high school seniors who score above 700 on both the verbal and the quantitative SAT tests. I am pleased to announce that half of those are admitted to Harvard." In many ways having generous academic and financial resources eases an institution's encounter with realities of the outside world.

pressure. Chancellor Heyman, who took office at Berkeley in 1980, announced that in addition to raising large sums of money for new buildings, endowed chairs, and general support, he would make it a major objective to ethnically diversify the campus without lowering the quality of our students or our academic programs.

In 1984 the Asian admission crisis was generated when the College of Letters and Science, under great application pressure, raised its minimum high school required-course GPA requirement for freshman admission without raising the standardized SAT (Scholastic Aptitude Test) score minima. This move was determined to have disadvantaged the Asian American applicants, contributing to a one-year drop in Asian and Asian American admissions of about 1 percentage point. Was Berkeley, by design, lowering the number of Asian American students in the freshman class, and if not, what policy had led to the decrease? This question led to the attorney general's investigation of the Berkeley admissions process and the campus response that was the topic of general policy discussion in the regents' November 1987 meeting.

The November 1987 Regents' Meeting

Ordinarily, our chancellor would have attended that regents meeting, given the report, and answered questions. But he and the Vice Chancellor for Student Affairs were about to depart on a fundraising trip to the Far East, and saw no difficulty in sending me to give what was to be a brief status report on how the Berkeley campus was responding to the criticism of the Asian American community. Two of us went to the meeting, the manager of the Admissions and Records Office, Bud Travers, who was the author of the Berkeley response to the Asian American concerns, and I. In theory, I would speak generally to the Asian issue, and Bud Travers would answer technical questions

111

about the admissions process in response to the report he had written and circulated to the regents. Before the meeting, I met with Regent Yori Wada, and we went over my presentation. It looked as though the bases were covered, but the discussion quickly came unraveled once the meeting began.

I presented the latest admissions data from the Berkeley campus, and Regent Wada responded that he was satisfied with the directions that Berkeley was taking. Dean Watkins and William French Smith, two of the conservative regents, then started a line of questioning that I was unable to respond to in detail, but hoped that Bud would be able to handle. They said to him, "We have reviewed your paper on how Berkeley admits freshmen and note that once half the class has been admitted on grades and test scores alone, you use other criteria. For the most part these criteria are objective and have yes or no answers. For example: Is an applicant a resident of the state of California? Has the student taken honors courses? Is the student from a rural high school? But there is one category that is weighted heavily that appears to be subjective, the essay," they said. "For those applicants whose essays are read, exactly how are they graded?"

Regent Dean Watkins then elaborated, "I have a question or two in relation to the supplementary criteria that are described in the report. There is a total of 1,300 points, and if you look at this list of seven categories, the first six are totally objective. In other words, there is no judgmental factor involved. Either you are a California resident or you are not. Either you're in EOP or you're not, and so on down the list, until you get to item seven, which is 500 points and is in fact five different things. Now, if I were a high school student, and wanted to attend Berkeley when I graduated, I'd want to know a lot more about what I had to do to pick up some or all of those 500 points. I wonder if we might have a detailed description of how 500 points are divided among those five categories, and what precisely the student is expected to do to earn those 500 points" The board chair, Regent Stanley Sheinbaum, then took up the questioning: "One of the things that's always bothered me about this admission process is how you monitor the essays and how you grade those, so if you're going to speak to that subject, I'd like to hear a brief discussion on how you go about evaluating essays, because this seems to be a problem that is constantly brought to my attention. The students who are applying just do not know what we are seeking and whether we have any objective method of evaluating the essays and how we are certain that they are in fact contributed by the students themselves as distinguished from someone else. I had not anticipated this, I would appreciate it."*

Bud Travers began a diffuse and wandering response. My heart sank when it became apparent that he did not have detailed answers to the regents' questions but didn't have the sense to know it, admit his ignorance, and promise to get back to them. The ensuing exchange was fueled by Bud's inability to say, "I don't know." Once the regents sensed his confusion, they became like sharks in a feeding frenzy, and the casualty was the credibility of the Berkeley freshman admissions process. We were being attacked by the Asian American community for allegedly discriminating illegally against Asian American applicants, and those in charge couldn't satisfactorily explain the admissions process. Worse yet, instead of admitting we didn't have a detailed answer to their questions, we, represented by Bud's performance, pretended to answer when we didn't know the answer. That Bud kept talking expanded the regents' perception of our incompetence—in retrospect a justified conclusion. After forty-five minutes of detailed questions for which there were no satisfactory answers, President Gardner said, "If

---

* These quotations, from a transcript of the Nov. 18–19, 1987 Regents' meeting, were provided by the Office of the Secretary of the Regents of the University of California.

this board of regents cannot thoroughly understand this process after this explanation, how do we expect the high school counselors to properly advise the students to make applications which really do justice to them?" Our ship was now filled to the gunwales and was about to go under.

The meeting had been a bloodbath. As we walked out, Bud, self-confident and oblivious to the disaster, asked, "Rod, I have to catch a plane for my Mexican vacation; may I take the rental car back to the airport?" I handed him the keys, thinking *good riddance—how can we possibly recover?*

Lunch was a traumatic experience. I was now contaminated property, and no one wished to get too close to it. If tribal societies have perfected punishment by shunning, the attendees at this lunch were no exception. Their reaction only strengthened my resolve to get back to Berkeley and get to the bottom of what was going on in the admissions process.

What had gone wrong with admissions? The answer is that administratively something had been going wrong for a number of years, and the administration had been too busy to notice it. The policies on admissions had become year-to-year responses to rapidly increasing numbers of applicants without recognizing that the policy of protected admissions for qualified minority applicants could not be defended under this competitive pressure.

The Recovery

With the Vice Chancellor for Undergraduate Affairs in Japan, and his manager of admissions in Mexico, I called up their staffs and started our recovery effort. I dropped almost all my other duties, and, with Patrick Hayashi, an administrative intern with the chancellor and one of the coordinators of ethnic studies with whom I had first worked fifteen years earlier, spent six solid weeks getting to the bottom of admissions. Once we had explicitly recorded the process for grading the application essays and distributed it to the president and to the regents, we started on the rest of the process and its history. Almost every meeting brought new surprises. For example, we had reported our admissions data for the fall semester only. In fact, about 1,000 freshmen accepted deferred admission for the spring semester, and they were almost entirely Caucasian and Asian American and were not in the data submitted to the regents. This fact was known neither to the administration nor to the Asian American community. Halfway through our review, Assemblyman Tom Hayden announced that he was holding hearings on Berkeley admissions in early February and requested that the chancellor testify. We were fortunate that our analysis was nearing completion, so the chancellor could be confident of his facts.

During January 1988, as I was completing the analysis for the chancellor's presentation at the Hayden hearing, I was contacted by the chair of the Ethnic Studies Department and invited to an informal meeting with the co-chairs of the Asian-American Task Force, Judges Ken Kawaichi and Lillian Sing. Sitting at a large round table in the private dining room of a Chinese restaurant in Jack London Square on the Oakland estuary, I told them what our intensive review had revealed about undergraduate admissions, including our shortcomings, and responded to questions.

It was evident that they had been distrustful of the Berkeley representatives they had dealt with before on this issue, and they were initially very cautious with me. I was not defensive. I told them exactly what had happened and that I was certain of the data that sustained our analysis. I countered their demands that the individuals responsible for the reduction in Asian American admissions in 1984 be fired, by arguing what I believed and still believe, that the fluctuations in the number of Asian American and other students had not been a matter of design, but more likely a matter of ignorance. In retrospect, our conversation was a good example that wherever two parties are on the scale of trust and distrust, their feelings about each other are almost always mutual. By the end of our discussion, the level of trust on both sides was increasing. That afternoon we began mending the wall that had been built between the Asian American community and the campus, a rebuilding that would not be finished for more than a year.

By late January 1988, we had prepared our report. The chancellor was on solid ground in his testimony when he issued an apology to the Asian community. At the January 26 hearing he said:

> ...I would like to say I wish that I had been more sensitive to the underlying concerns at issue. While they did not manifest themselves as neatly as I now see them, Berkeley could have reacted more openly and less defensively than we did. Because the anxieties were elevated, I apologize for this. I really do believe that regardless of the occasional hostilities between the Task Force and the campus, that the Task Force has performed a very good service in opening up all of these issues for a vote, for viewing and debate.[*]

He went on to enumerate the studies and structural changes the campus was making to prevent the situation from recurring in the future.

Assemblyman Hayden then responded, "Thank you, Mr. Chancellor, for a remarkable statement. I appreciate it. Your statement, as I heard it, acknowledged mistakes, lack of sensitivity, and lack of participation. I know it's not easy to make these sorts of statements. There is no one in this room that has always been sensitive to every new demand or issue."

The Asian-American Task Force, as might be expected, took a wait and see attitude. It was not until April 6, 1989, a year later,

---

[*] Excerpts from California Legislature Hearing, State Capitol, Jan 26, 1988, 0216-A.

in the same restaurant where I had started our communication with the Asian Task Force, that Chancellor Heyman and Judges Ken Kawaichi and Lillian Sing, co-chairs of the Asian-American Task Force on University Admissions, issued a joint statement* that Berkeley had taken "important steps toward responding and has engaged in developing new procedures and policies that would ensure fairness and provide reassurance to the Asian community."

We were warned that publishing exactly how the Berkeley campus admits freshmen was what no other major university had ever done. We were further warned that telling people exactly how we admitted freshmen would only compound our difficulties. Our critics were wrong! Once our process was publicized, my telephone stopped ringing, and the discussion moved to a higher-level policy debate. The balancing of a color- and culture-blind admission process with sound public policy has no absolute answer, and the parade of parents whose children apply each year for freshman status must work through the issues again. New marchers in this parade will find that the balancing of a strictly formulaic academic meritocracy on the one hand, with what makes sound public policy for California on the other, is not an easy question and that people of good faith come up with different positions. The extent to which it is good public policy for a state university to take factors other than grades and test scores into account for admissions is a topic on which there is little agreement.

At the base of the argument are three issues. First there is the use of the university for addressing issues of perceived social inequity. With respect to race this issue was decided by voter-approved Proposition 209, which disallows any consideration of race in admissions by the University of California. Second there is the range of qualities we look for in applicants, and third, the question of how we weigh them. Particularly in the multicultural

---

* Reported in *The New York Times,* May 25, 1989.

society of California this debate will continue. Freshman admission in an overenrolled public university is a problem that can only be answered in the context of a given time, consistent with the way in which our society views its objectives.

In the twenty years since the Asian American admission issue surfaced at Berkeley, the Asian American freshman population has continued to increase because of the high eligibility and high acceptance rate of these students. Of 4,107 freshmen who enrolled at the University of California at Berkeley in fall 2007, 46.7 percent were Asian Americans and 30.8 percent were Caucasian.

Chapter 10

Lesson 2 – Reorganization of Biology

The Shortest Distance between Two Points is Not Always a Straight Line

Reorganizing the biological sciences at Berkeley appears from some accounts to have been a five- or ten-year process that began in the late 1970s. In reality, the seeds of reorganization were sown in the early 1960s by a group of young faculty members from the Zoology, Botany, and Biochemistry Departments. Under the initial leadership of plant biochemist David Hackett, this group met informally to discuss the plethora of introductory biology courses on the Berkeley campus, each as the introduction to a departmental major. Botany 1, Zoology 1A and 1B, and Bacteriology 1 were all taught from a departmental perspective, with an increasing amount of material (genetics and metabolism, for example) becoming common to all. Our group, which consisted of David Hackett, Fred Wilt, Dick Strohman, Oscar Paris, and me, later joined by Robert Haynes, Gunther Stent, John Gerhart, Morgan Harris, and Daniel Branton, began to question whether biology at Berkeley was administratively and intellectually structured to take maximum advantage of the rapidly developing field of molecular biology as applied to the biosphere in all its dimensions.

Berkeley was founded as a campus in 1868, only nine years after Charles Darwin published *On the Origin of Species*. Its initial departments, reflecting the new evolutionary thinking, were established along evolutionary lines. The Botany, Zoology, and Entomology Departments were soon followed by departments that cut across the early disciplines, reflecting developments in physiology, genetics, biochemistry, virology, and finally molecular biology.

The activities of our initial group, the Biology 1 Committee, resulted in a 1963 report to the Biology Council (a group consisting of chairmen of all the Berkeley biology departments) recommending that all the existing introductory courses in botany, zoology, and bacteriology be combined into a new unified year-long course to emphasize the new unity in biology that was becoming apparent through elucidation of the genetic code and a realization of the great chemical similarities among all organisms. The Biology Council accepted our recommendation. It obtained the money from the administration to remodel four large teaching laboratories, support space, and a large lecture hall, and gave five of us the responsibility to offer the course for the first time in fall 1966, a time that coincided with the blossoming of the student movement. Excitement and enthusiasm accompanied our new undertaking.

We all attended each other's lectures in room 2000 Life Sciences Building (LSB) at 8:00 a.m. for the entire year. Each laboratory contained a library of the classic books that marked the intellectual history of biology. Our experiments ranged from the classical dissection of the frog to the Delbruck-Luria fluctuation test, observation of cytochromes in the flight muscles of insects, and field observation on populations of California voles, to experiments in neurobiology. This course and the Department of Instruction in Biology that sustained it and other interdepartmental biology offerings was, in retrospect, a first step toward the extensive reorganization of biology programs at Berkeley that would follow twenty years later.

By the end of the 1960s, two important events had occurred that influenced future developments in the biological programs. First, Berkeley had reached its maximum number of students and therefore its maximum faculty size under the regental policy at that time. New biological fields could no longer be accommodated by adding new departments populated by new faculty based on increasing enrollments. Second, remarkable events in molecular biology were about to change the face of biological research. The discovery of techniques for cloning foreign DNA in bacteria, the ability to identify specific clones that coded specific proteins, and the ability to determine the base sequence of DNA responsible for coding specific proteins, all occurred over a ten-year period between 1970 and 1980.

During this period, in 1972, I became the Provost and Dean of the College of Letters and Science. Under the bylaws of the Academic Senate, the College of Letters and Science has an Executive Committee that serves as the college Educational Policy Committee. Following one of their meetings in fall 1973, we adjourned to the bar of the Faculty Club. At that time, Marian ("Bunny") Koshland, a professor of microbiology, served on the Executive Committee. Her husband, professor of biochemistry Daniel Koshland, joined us at a central table, and we began to discuss the future of biology at Berkeley. Both Dan and Bunny strongly asserted that new currents in molecular biology, the discovery of restriction enzymes that specifically cleave DNA, development of DNA sequencing techniques, and recombinant DNA technology were opening up enormous research areas in biology in which Berkeley, because of its aging facilities and traditional departmental structures, was not going to compete well. They were convinced that Berkeley would drop in the next round of graduate rankings of biology (as did happen), and that I should undertake a major restructuring of both our physical plant and intellectual organization as reflected by departmental missions.

This discussion reinforced a discomfort I had felt on a number of occasions when I observed that our younger biology faculty members from many different biology departments were meeting in the Faculty Club to hold seminars on cell and molecular biology. It was painfully evident that our present academic organization was not meeting the intellectual needs of the very people who were the future of biology at Berkeley.

I was quietly agonized by my discussion with the Koshlands because I knew they were correct. At the same time, the inertia against which change must press seemed insurmountable. My responsibility as curator for the health of academic departments in the College of Letters and Science following the malaise of the 1960s was intimidating to begin with. Adding a problem of this magnitude, at a time when the political and economic climate of the state of California under Governor Reagan was unfavorable to new initiatives, led me to short-lived depression before it led to resolve.

I considered this challenge consciously and unconsciously for several weeks, and then, with Fred Carpenter, the Divisional Dean of Biology, came up with a strategy. We would start with an inventory of all biologists on the Berkeley campus, categorized by research interest rather than by existing departments or college so we could realistically assess the strengths of our faculty resource regardless of departmental or college affiliation. This tactic had several advantages. In the initial stages it was non-threatening and involved the entire biology faculty. Faculty members are busy people and often regard administrative requests in their mailboxes as so much administrative snow, to be shoveled away as soon as possible. But an administrative draft describing the faculty member's research area and requesting editing is likely to gain immediate and solicitous attention of even the most withdrawn professor.

At this point, any suggestion of reorganization of departments to meet changing directions in the fields of biology would have been soundly rejected. To begin, it is almost impossible to discontinue an academic unit of a university. Pressures for continuance of departments come from alumni, who feel that the value of their degree, and hence their own value, will be diminished. Pressures for continuance also come from students, from their parents, and from professional societies, often through their legislative representatives. In addition, faculty tenure conspires against foreclosure of an academic program in what would be a routine process for industry. At a senate meeting, one of our faculty members captured this dilemma well. He said somewhat whimsically, "If this campus had been founded early enough to have a Department of Alchemy, I'm sure it would still exist!" If outright discontinuance of a unit is not possible, evolution and change is. A strategy of program evolution encouraged by appropriate inducements is the path of effective program change in the easily perturbed collegial environment. If a weak academic unit with tenure faculty is reorganized, it is important that tenure faculty be dispersed among strong disciplined units who will enforce new, increased standards for evaluation. A nucleus of weak faculty members transferred en masse to a new department usually transmits the weakness also. When receiving departments resist, remind them that tenure has obligations as well as benefits.

The inventory of biology faculty members, categorized by research area or "intellectual affinity groups," was completed in the mid-1970s. It was followed by two studies: a review of our total biology program and a review of our facilities. The first study reviewed our faculty inventory to assess our strengths and to decide where overall campus resources should be emphasized or reduced. The faculty members for this study were carefully chosen to include a preponderance of the younger tenured biologists who represented Berkeley's future, as well as some of the senior citizens of the biology community. This first report, which appeared in 1980, recommended that six areas—immunology, neurobiology, population biology and applied ecology, molecular plant biology, endocrinology and structure, and organization and function of the eucaryotic genome—receive specific attention in the reorganization. In early 1981, following our internal review of the inventory of faculty and choosing academic areas for emphasis, we established a national review committee.* This committee was to advise us on our progress toward reorganizing biology, and to make recommendations about the directions that we were taking. Specific appointments to the review committee were critical to the success of our efforts. First, our faculty was likely to listen to an external committee of their peers that they had helped select. Internal committees and the administration could never carry as much weight. Second, and this only became evident years later, members of an external committee who help create a major change at Berkeley through their studies and reports have made an investment in the campus, making some of them ambassadors for recruitment to Berkeley. Little did I realize that the external committee, in addition to its other good work, was a useful recruitment device.

The first external committee report was received in April 1981. Remarking on the current status of biological sciences at Berkeley, the committee noted that "there has been a notable decline in national standing over the past 30 years. This decline reflects a failure to cope adequately with the revolutionary changes that have occurred since the early 1950s. At that earlier time, the haphazard department organization was roughly congruent with the research and instruction programs in the

---

* The committee members were John Abelson, Professor of Chemistry, UC San Diego; Robert Barker (Chairman), Director, Division of Biological Sciences, Cornell; David Botstein, Professor of Genetics, MIT; G. Bush, Professor of Biology, University of Texas, Austin; William Dawson, Chairman, Division of Biological Sciences, University of Michigan; George Palade, Professor of Cell Biology, Yale University; Peter Raven, Director of the Missouri Botanical Garden; S. J. Singer, Professor of Biology U.C. San Diego; and S. van Gundy, Professor of Nematology, UC Riverside.

area. These strongly emphasized the diversity of biology. This organizational pattern no longer fits with the perceived universalities of biology. The departmental organization at Berkeley now inhibits the free flow of information, the development of collaborative teaching and research efforts and the exploration of the interfaces where many of the new discoveries have been made." The committee found that "UC Berkeley is notable among major institutions in the United States in housing most of its biology programs in substandard buildings. They do not meet safety regulations, and it is doubtful that even a complete renovation could bring them to the appropriate standard."

The third major criticism, and the one that I was least successful in addressing, was "The complexity of the administrative arrangements affecting biology at UC Berkeley is impressive. Authority and responsibility is diffused and the administrative chain-of-command is excessively long. ... All of the faculty who teach and do research in the biological sciences should belong to the same administrative structure."

One of the empirical rules in chapter 14 is "If you are going to leap a chasm, don't do it in two steps." Unfortunately, reorganization at Berkeley fell half a step short. The College of Natural Resources, formerly the College of Agriculture, except for several professors of genetics, and the Department of Plant Molecular Biology stood apart from the new departmental structures and programs. The College of Natural Resources faculty had eleven-month appointments and federal agricultural funds (Hatch Act) that they felt might be jeopardized by participating in the reorganization. Non-participation served that college poorly in subsequent years as their enrollments dropped in relation to the biology enrollments in participating units. That the College of Natural Resources did not participate was actually a political relief to the rest of the campus and particularly the College of Letters and Science, because an amalgamation would, de facto, have created a College of Biology pulling almost one hundred faculty members from L&S. But the continued separation assured a long road of tensions and inefficiencies for campus biology programs.

An essential recommendation of the review committee was implemented: establishment of a strong advisory council of intellectual leaders among the biology faculty, who would work closely with the provosts on all matters of program areas, faculty recruitment authorizations in relation to program priorities, space, charges to review committees, and coordination of teaching programs.

Finally, the review committee agreed with the campus that "The reorganization of biology programs should proceed sufficiently rapidly so that new space can be designed to meet the needs of reorganized rather than traditional units. If this is not done, and the buildings are designed in relation to existing departments, it will be exceedingly difficult to change and accommodate the much needed affinity groupings of faculty members." This recommendation was consistent with our primary strategy for modernizing biology at Berkeley: create new spaces and fill them with intellectual affinity groups rather than the traditional departments.

A second study was a parallel architectural study carried out by the planners Kaplan, McLaughlin, and Diaz in the early 1980s to determine what options, including remodeling and new space, were available for providing proper modern space compatible with biology-program directions, particularly those using the new techniques of molecular and cell biology. This study set the general plan for three major developments: the construction of an annex to the existing Life Sciences Building (LSA); the construction of a new building near the Biochemistry Building; and remodeling of the Life Sciences Building itself to house the botanical, zoological, and paleontological collections and the systematists, population biologists and ecologists who make use of them.

Why Berkeley Had a Unique Opportunity

By the early 1980s, the prospect was exciting. We had a unique opportunity, because Berkeley's great existing strengths in the organismal and evolutionary fields of botany, zoology, microbiology, entomology, and paleontology would be enriched by use of the exciting new techniques of cell and molecular biology. Although many other research universities rushed to exploit the new techniques, they often did not have Berkeley's intimate knowledge of the biosphere, collections from it, and therefore a way to determine what important problems might be addressed by the new techniques. I have often warned students to know more than just the techniques of molecular biology—also know enough about the biosphere and the organisms in it to recognize the important problems. Otherwise, I warned them, "you may become like the radio amateur with tens of thousands of dollars of equipment and nothing to say."

When I became vice chancellor in the administration of Chancellor Ira Michael Heyman in the fall of 1980, one of the first tasks Heyman set for us was to draw up a set of priorities for Berkeley's first formal fund drive. Though we were new at the fundraising game, we knew that, to be achieved, our goals must be directly related to the maintenance and extension of academic excellence, which over the years has been the reason most new students give as their primary reason for attending UC Berkeley. We met several times with the provosts and deans as we developed our list. The end result, though not surprising, was certified by these efforts. We would ask for one hundred endowed chairs for retention and recruitment of faculty, ongoing research support, and a mix of departmental and graduate-student support under a heading I particularly enjoyed suggesting, "CAL Futures," as it signified an investment for the future that would increase in value. Buildings for business administration and engineering were also on our list, but the centerpiece was three buildings for the biological sciences. These had a price tag of $155 million, $47 million of which would have to be raised from private sources. How this enormous project became certified as the fundraising centerpiece—in competition with the building aspirations of the business school, engineering college, and several other programs—resulted largely from a recognition by faculty members that the national rankings of our biology departments were probably going to slip markedly, and that these departments exhibited the greatest need for academic invigoration and support. Several professors commented that they didn't wish to belong to a campus that benignly tolerated central academic programs slipping in distinction, particularly in fields undergoing revolutionary changes. Thus biology became certified as the focus of our fundraising campaign for sound academic reasons.

The obligation of the Berkeley campus to raise $47 million privately toward the biology projects was the outcome of a discussion the chancellor and I had with President David Gardner in 1981 on the amount of assistance we could expect from the state capital budget. We learned rapidly that our need for $155 million for biology reorganization at Berkeley could not be expected from the state, given the budgetary needs of the other eight campuses of the university. Could we make up part of the difference between expected state funding and our need from fundraising in the private sector? President Gardner was initially reluctant to allow us to raise any private funds toward buildings that sustained the regular instructional program, because such construction had been a traditional obligation of the state of California. To start funding such buildings privately might set a precedent that could be very dangerous to future capital programs of the university. The legislature, Gardner speculated, in their efforts to spread limited tax revenues as widely as possible, might view such private fundraising as applicable to all capital projects for the university, something the newer campuses could not hope to accomplish.

It was also unclear how private universities such as Stanford would respond to Berkeley entering the competition for private funds on a large scale. Chancellor Heyman was particularly effective in countering this latter argument when he pointed out that only about half of the Berkeley yearly budget at that time came from the state of California, whereas about half the Stanford budget came from the federal government. In Heyman's words, "Berkeley is among the best state-assisted universities while Stanford is one of the best federally assisted universities."

As Chancellor Heyman and I walked out of President Gardner's office, the vastness of what we had agreed to overtook us. Neither of us had ever thought of raising a sum as large as $47 million for "bricks and mortar," which is hardly the favorite object of foundation giving. Now we had wagered the reputation of the Berkeley campus on the odds that we could be successful, and neither of us could claim experience as a large-scale fundraiser. Like my first job as a graduate student, in which I confidently declared that I could operate a machine lathe, economic necessity proved a powerful inducement for skill acquisition, especially by the chancellor.

We were warned by colleagues from other academic institutions that, as newcomers, we could not expect donors to fund what we were interested in; they would fund only what they were interested in. Only universities such as Harvard or Princeton, they maintained, could dictate the direction of donors' funds. Fortunately, eight years of effort on the part of Chancellor Heyman showed our critics were wrong. A total of $470 million was raised during that first campaign and its extension through June 1990. The $47 million goal for biology buildings was met and exceeded.

Although many individuals and foundations contributed toward that goal, two $15 million gifts were the essential underpinning for our success. The first gift came from the Wayne and Gladys Valley Foundation, which was set up on the death of Wayne, a developer and an original owner of the Oakland

Raiders football team, for educational purposes. The second $15 million gift came from philanthropists Gordon and Ann Getty, who had become closer to Berkeley over the Heyman years partly through Gordon Getty's interest in Berkeley's anthropological programs on human evolution, and also through Ann Getty's matriculation as a Berkeley undergraduate during this period. These gifts, both received during the 1989–90 academic year, assured that the major revitalization of Berkeley biology would be completed.

An empirical number arose at this time concerning the relationship of Berkeley's fundraising efforts compared with those of Stanford: Berkeley's fundraising goals for each comparable effort would be about one third of Stanford's. Independently, our initial campaign goal was set at $312 million while Stanford set its goal at $1.1 billion. Endowed professorial chairs at Berkeley, by regents' policy, cost a minimum of $400,000, whereas at Stanford the cost was over $1 million; and of the total cost of $155 million for the three Berkeley biology capital projects, President Gardner determined that the Berkeley campus should raise $47 million, or about one third of the total. I do not believe the correspondence among these percentages was noticed until all the determinations had been made.

By the spring of 1984, the Chancellor's Advisory Committee on Biology (the advisory council recommended in the external review) had produced a final iteration of the proposed reorganization of biology for consideration by the faculty.[*] That same spring, the first building of our ambitious three-building plan for biology was before the California legislature for budgetary approval. Thus, the future intellectual road map of biology for Berkeley, and the incentive for its implementation, new facilities, were under consideration at the same time, and approval of either was far from certain.

---

[*] Professor Daniel Koshland and Louise Taylor played essential roles in this process.

Faculty Consideration of the Biological Sciences Reorganization

For many Berkeley students, Sproul Plaza is the center of campus. This is not so for the faculty. For them the center is a quiet, sylvan spot known as Faculty Glade. No building has been allowed to intrude on it since the Faculty Club, designed by the renowned Berkeley architect Bernard Maybeck, was constructed at the east end of the glade in 1903. In prehistoric times, Faculty Glade, bisected by Strawberry Creek and sheltered by large California live oaks, was the site of an Ohlone Indian encampment, whose tribal rituals were undoubtedly as complex and serious as those of the present inhabitants.

The Faculty Club itself is a rambling, two-story redwood and shingled building with porches for outside dining. Its centerpiece is a great hall, at one time reserved for members only, conceived in the medieval traditions of northern Europe. A ridge two stories tall is supported by steeply pitched redwood beams that are supported in turn by horizontal members whose interior ends are carved as mythical creatures who preside over the hall. These horizontal members are supported by large vertical redwood beams that frame coats of arms skillfully executed in stained glass. The walls are decorated with the mounted heads of large wild animals. The largest of these is a moose head, which has become the icon of the club and appears on all its formal correspondence.

Several years ago, members of animal rights groups requested that the animal heads be removed from the hall, serving in their view as a barbaric reminder of man's inhumanity to beasts. The directors, with uncommon wit, transferred this issue to the members of the club for response. Their request stimulated a creative flurry by the faculty whose responses ranged from scholarly defenses based on historic arguments to the observation, "Why, if we have a policy of removing stuffed heads, we will have to remove half the members!"

131

But back to the hall itself. Whereas the east end is open through windows to the sky, the west end is occupied by an enormous baronial stone fireplace lit only on such occasions as the Christmas feast. The feast commences when an authentically dressed monks' chorus carries an enormous boar's head through the hall while rendering an a cappella performance of "The Boar's Head Carol." In January 1984, this great hall with all its traditions was the site of the first general meeting of the biology faculty with the administration to discuss the merits and demerits of reorganizing biology at Berkeley.

Early in 1984, standing in front of the fireplace in the Great Hall, I faced some 125 biology faculty members who had come to discuss the first reorganization plan for biology. I knew there would be expressions of hope, anger, enthusiasm, and skepticism, and I was not disappointed. Following my introduction, which traced the major threads of the biological reorganization issues of the previous ten years, three consecutive speakers told us that we were among the best, if not the best, biology program in the country and that changes were unnecessary. After all our efforts, was this the true sentiment of the faculty? I began to feel as though I was becoming trapped in an enormous, viscous bowl of academic oatmeal as the speakers droned on. But the fourth speech, from a younger member of the faculty, questioned the complacency (recall Robert Byron p. 17) of the prior speakers and suggested that we should be looking to the future rather than the past. The ebb and flow of argument continued until hunger pangs or desire for pre-dinner libations won out. We agreed to hold further meetings during the spring.

At the next meeting in the Faculty Club library, a pragmatic objection arose to which I had no truly satisfactory answer. Why, the question went, are we going to all this trouble when we don't even know whether the California legislature will approve the capital funds necessary to initiate the facilities? By this time the Chancellor's Advisory Council had produced a second iteration for a reorganization of biology on the Berkeley campus. It produced fewer strong objections, but the plan was not strongly endorsed, pending the outcome of the legislative budget hearings on the new building.

I wondered whether it would ever be possible to get movement on the reorganization proposal. As I look back on the spring of 1984, we needed both the buildings and the reorganization—and we had neither. We seemed to have a huge locomotive stalled on the tracks. It was foolish to think that I alone could initiate action.

The first real movement came as a result of the legislative committee hearings. Our proposals for new biology facilities were opposed by the staff of the Legislative Analyst's office both on program grounds (this amount of space per faculty member and per student would exceed the standards set for biology in 1950) and because there was considerable doubt that the campus could raise the nearly $50 million in private funds required to complete the projects. Could we guarantee that we could raise the money and would not be back to the legislature to beg for the money we were unable to raise? But the legislators themselves looked beyond the staff concerns to a much livelier issue, the issue of animal care on the Berkeley campus. The decision to fund our projects would finally be decided, not on the academic merits of our proposal, but on the Berkeley campus response to the animal care issue.

The Animal Care Issue in 1984

Until the early 1980s, care of laboratory animals was largely in the hands of individual investigators and was carried on in departmentally controlled space. The faculty researchers had been trained by their own mentors, and the result was extraordinarily uneven husbandry practices affecting a range of activities from surgery to cage cleaning and the training of animal technicians and graduate students. In 1981, our first provost for research, George Maslach, asked the national accrediting group of veterinarians, the American Association for Laboratory Animal Care (AALAC), to pay the campus an inspection visit and advise us on how to improve our facilities and practices. We were not aware that AALAC performed only accreditation visits, and didn't just provide advice.

To our amazement, in July 1982, we received "provisional accreditation" with a long list of facility, management, and training deficiencies that were to be corrected by a mandatory follow-up visit in late 1983, when we would either become fully accredited or lose our provisional accreditation. Provisional accreditation, it turned out, was not a blessing. The second AALAC visit was preceded by a flurry of activity to clean facilities and to outline some programs for management improvement, but it was not enough. On February 2, 1984, while we were considering the reorganization and arguing for funding before the legislature, Chancellor Heyman received a letter from AALAC informing him that the AALAC Council on Accreditation had decided to withhold accreditation. Improvements were noted in the physical plant, number of professional staff, sanitation, and animal identification, but the inspectors were dissatisfied with overall direction and planning and our rate of progress. The decentralized nature of faculty research, coupled with a few people who were not about to change their methods because they had "always done it this way," was about to cause the end of the biology reorganization before it had even started.

The denial of accreditation was much more than one more nail in the coffin of biology reorganization. It was the ideal issue for animal rights enthusiasts to parade before the legislature during budgetary hearings as they opposed a new biology facility at Berkeley. We expected that a challenge from the animal rights groups would occur after our experience with the hearings on the environmental impact report for the first biology building

Life Science Annex (LSA) in 1982. At that hearing the activists had argued that the EIR report was insufficient because it did not consider the kinds of research proposed for the building, in particular animal research. This argument, which established a new theory of law that environmental impact reports should evaluate not only the structure and its impact on the environment, but also the functions within it, had fortunately been rejected.

We had three strikes against biology reorganization in spring 1984: the reluctance of the faculty to reorganize; the negative views of the legislative analyst; and the attack of the animal rights groups on any new biology facilities for Berkeley.

It soon became apparent that state funding for LSA, the first of the three buildings required for the biology reorganization, would not be decided on the merits of our biology program, but rather on whether Berkeley had in place a plan to gain accreditation for its animal research. Knowing the importance of this issue, we searched for a consultant veterinarian who could help us and settled on the old-time, experienced, and politically savvy DVM Albert ("Al") G. Edward. Al went right to work and visited all the facilities, spoke with the animal care technicians, chided the faculty, and advised the administration.[*]

We can speculate about why this issue arose when it did.

---

[*] Before the recent interest in legal and moral rights of animals, veterinarians did not have high visibility in American political society. Except for occasional stories of foot and mouth disease migrating north from Mexico, and cat leukemia scares, veterinarians seldom engaged in debates on public policy. Why all this changed is a matter of speculation. In ancient times, every leader was accompanied by a bodyguard and shaman, who respectively protected the leader from attack and ordained the future. The leaders of today are accompanied by their lawyers and their economists for much the same purposes. But the emergence of an animal rights movement required an additional talent for leaders of research institutions. If leaders were to appear at hearings, they now had to be accompanied by a third party—veterinarians alone could certify whether an institution was in compliance with federal and state law on standards for animal care, a matter that became an increasingly prominent legislative concern during the 1980s.

One observation is that concern about child abuse and animal care are parallel issues. For the past one hundred years, concern about these issues as measured by lines in the public press have increased and decreased together. Thirty years ago animal welfare was not a great concern in the United States but was a major public concern in Great Britain. The word among animal physiologists used to be, "If you want to work on animals, go to the United States. If you want to work on people, go to Great Britain." In any case, the so-called animal rights movement was particularly well established in California in the mid-1980s, and, like any emerging social concern, received attention from the legislature, an institution whose members' survival is often based on sensitive response to new trends. The movement itself was not broadly based either ethnically or socioeconomically. It is typically the concern of a white, middle-to-upper-class constituency. Some Blacks and Chicanos at Berkeley were heard to say, "To hell with the animals, what about us?"

But it must be remembered that, in California where only 40 percent of eligible voters go to the polls, it is the largely white upper middle class who vote and contribute funds to election campaigns. If our legislators weren't listening to E. F. Hutton in the spring of 1984, they were listening to well-placed animal rights advocates. This is the political climate under which the hearings for our first building, the Life Sciences Annex, were held.

Legislative Hearings on the Animal Issue

The California legislature has two houses, the State Assembly and the Senate. Over the years, the most contentious hearings on the university budget, and particularly the capital budget, have occurred in the Assembly's Ways and Means Subcommittee hearings. The subcommittee is generally composed of six members, equally divided among Republicans and Democrats. These hearings have always been a high-stakes game for the university. A capital project that has survived university staff review and has made its way into both the regents' and governor's budget can, because of an offhand remark, lack of a good one-liner at the right time, or failure to lobby the members effectively before the hearing, or just because of a member's bad mood, fail to pass in the subcommittee and face an uncertain future. The game for the university is then all downside risk. The power of the subcommittee over the university is based more on its ability to withhold projects than to approve them. This is the dynamic that faced the first biology project in the spring of 1984.

The animal rights groups had lobbied the subcommittee members long and hard against our projects. They had support from many Hollywood donors to the legislators' political campaigns as well as the political lobbying skill of Gladys Sergeant (heiress to Sergeant's Flea and Tick Powder). Gladys spent a great deal of time walking the legislative halls reminding the solons of her contributions to their political campaigns. Sergeant, unlike some of her earnest, anguished, and humorless radical colleagues, was a confident, jovial, and effective adversary. At the hearings she generally wore a large hat decorated with several long, handsome feathers, which always tempted me to ask, "Where did you get those feathers, Gladys?"

The chairman of the Assembly Ways and Means Subcommittee, Bob Campbell, was a local assemblyman who saw the political issue of animal rights to his advantage—providing he could emerge as a peacemaker between the two sides. A peaceful result would probably never emerge in the formal hearing, so at least two preliminary hearings were held to debate the issue. Subcommittee members at this time could "let the gas out of the balloon" and, with deep concern, listen and respond to the arguments in hopes of generating a compromise.

Following the first meeting, the chair retired to a local bar with some of us, and the discussion shifted to hobbies. The chair told us that to keep in top physical condition he practiced karate. In his enthusiasm he indicated he was not only fairly skillful, but was proud of his accomplishment. His enthusiasm continued as he explained his training regimen. "One of the most important advantages in karate comes from speed and quickness of hand-eye coordination. There are several ways to practice at home. "We often put goldfish in a tank and carefully lower our hand in the water and attempt to grab them without rippling the surface." Looking at a scratch on the back of his hand, he went on, "Another good technique is to slap the face of your cat and be able to withdraw your hand before the cat scratches you." Looking back, I wish the animal rightists had been there. So much for the relationship of political issues to our everyday life.

At the first preliminary hearing, Gladys Sergeant announced that our veterinary consultant, Al Edward, was as cruel and unsympathetic as the rest of us at the university. She had learned from an unquestioned source that Al was a hunter who actually shot and ate wild animals. This, she claimed, discredited our assertion that we were serious about improving animal care at Berkeley, and would be a point that she would emphasize at the formal hearing. A few days later the chancellor, his assistant, John Cummins, the Vice Chancellor for Research Chiang Lin Tien (subsequently chancellor of Berkeley), Al Edward, and I were again driving to Sacramento for a second informal hearing. During a lull in the conversation, John Cummins said to Al in a teasing tone, "Al, how could you have the gall to appear at a hearing on animal care at Berkeley when we have learned that you are a hunter and eat wild animals?" Al started one of his long haw-haws and, laughing all the while, said, "Yes, I am a hunter. I have shot wild animals and eaten them, and when I was in the army I shot men too." The shock of Al's gallows humor caused me to spurt out unnecessarily, "Don't ever say that at a hearing." Al glowed with a satisfaction that he had alarmed us.

His age and his recognition of the absurdity of the human condition had made us all look smaller.

KQED Debate

During this same contentious animal spring of 1984, the local Bay Area public television station, KQED, decided to offer a debate on the issue of animal research within the format of their thirty-minute *Express* program. There would be equal representation of views in a general format of ten minutes of introductory interviews and tapes, followed by a statement from a spokesperson from each side, and then questions from the audience. The chancellor of Berkeley was invited to present the pro-animal-research side. With his unerring political sense, Chancellor Heyman refused and instead offered his vice chancellor (me). This was not a task I relished, because I knew I would be debating a professional who made his living from arguing for animal rights. Also, I would be at a disadvantage because Berkeley does not have a medical school. I could not easily give examples of alleviating human suffering through therapies developed using animal research, and would not have testimonials from thankful patients. My role in this instance was much like that of Tom Wolfe's "flak catcher" in *Mau-Mauing the Flak Catchers.* In the "war on poverty" in the late '60s, the local agency director was always in Washington, and the second in command (in this case the vice chancellor) was left to fend off the political thrusts aimed at the director. So it was for *Express* in 1984 that I arrived at the KQED studio adjacent to the freeway in downtown San Francisco. I was directed to a green room where the professional debater, Michael Gianelli, was already confidently ensconced. He explained that he didn't wear leather shoes or belts and that his children were not vaccinated. I reminded him that a farmer in the Central Valley of California who chose not to treat his fields with pesticide was generally safe from insects because all the surrounding fields were sprayed. Perhaps his children were protected in the same way.

Shortly, we were directed to a stage backed by a projection screen facing an audience of several hundred, divided into equal parts on the basis of their views about the use of animals as research subjects. The program began with filmed interviews followed by movies of the United States Army blasting pigs with flamethrowers, and photographs of restrained primates undergoing what appeared to be very painful procedures. I began to get the drift, and I remembered what an old newspaperman in the campus Public Information Office, Dick Hafner, had told me years earlier: "There is no news in airplanes landing safely!" After ten minutes a color picture of the campanile, the tall bell tower that dominates the Berkeley campus, appeared on the screen. Simultaneously our host said, "There appear to be some very real problems in animal research on the Berkeley campus. Mr. Gianelli, what are those problems?" Gianelli then went on for another ten minutes about alleged atrocities to animals by Berkeley researchers, and why it would be a further atrocity for the legislature to fund a new biology building on the Berkeley campus that would house animal research. By now twenty minutes of negative comments about the campus had been registered, and the host finally asked me for a response.

Being "set up" deftly is one thing; being intentionally abused is something else. I didn't see how I could recover without some help from the animal activists themselves, so I plunged in. "What has preceded is a total misrepresentation of animal research at Berkeley. We do not work on pigs, we do not work on dogs, and about ninety-five percent of the animals used in research at Berkeley are mice, rats, and guinea pigs." I went on: "For example, we work on the reproduction of mosquitoes in the pools of water held in the crotches of California oak trees." I suddenly became aware that a large bearded man had left the animal activist side of the audience and was striding across the stage toward me. Immediately I recognized him as Eliot Katz, a former veterinarian from New York who left that profession and came to California, where he had tried several new activities including art presentations in San Francisco. But his final decision was to devote his efforts to the Animal Rights movement, and he founded "In Defense of Animals," now a multimillion-dollar-per-year business. He strode up, on live television, pointed his finger at me, and, with his beard quivering, shouted, "Vice Chancellor Park is a corrupt and blatant liar. He is personally responsible for the torture and murder of tens of thousands of animals each year at Berkeley." His diatribe, hardly the language of debate in the legislature and certainly not that of the Academic Senate, went on for about thirty seconds. The host was unable or unwilling to stop it, but Katz had given me the opening I needed. When he had finished, I looked out at the audience and said wistfully, taking the final line from *Some Like It Hot*, "Well, nobody's perfect!" The entire audience burst into laughter, and even Gladys Sergeant, the old-time animal activist and political organizer, joined in. The host had totally lost control by this time and was looking appropriately distraught. What did I learn from this experience?

Once you are badly set up, induce your enemy to save you!

The Final Hearings

The political impasse generated by the animal activists had the legislative subcommittee in an awkward position. If they did approve the building, they would appear either to have declared themselves as veterinarians and certified the Berkeley animal program, or, if they disapproved the building, to have again looked like veterinarians and decertified it. A consensus was reached that the Berkeley animal program should be reviewed by a third body that had credibility with all concerned. The group chosen for this review was the California Postsecondary

Education Commission, which at that time was headed by Pat Callan, an experienced staffer who had worked previously for Assemblyman John Vasconcellos. Pat Callan in turn assigned the review to his expert on health sciences, Dr. Rosyln Elms, former Dean of the Nursing School at Massachusetts General Hospital and a former legislative consultant in Sacramento. Roz Elms, a graduate of the program in Higher Education at the Berkeley School of Education, was known as a tough, independent-minded administrator who had the respect of both staff and members of the legislature. She came to Berkeley several times, toured our facilities, and interviewed many faculty members, students, professional staff, and the administration. She then retired to Sacramento to write her report.

This report and its reception would prove to be the pivotal event in our efforts to implement the biology reorganization. If the report were unfavorable, it would make it easy for the subcommittee to satisfy a vocal and well-to-do constituency, the animal activists, and to save the state an immediate expenditure of $40 million, both highly attractive legislative options. On the other hand, if the report found that the Berkeley campus was improving its training, management, and facilities for animal research, and recommended funding, we would not only get the building, we could also expect that academic reorganization and successful fundraising for the rest of the biology buildings in the campaign would follow. We heard nothing for about two weeks and awaited Roz's call with some anxiety. When it finally came, she had determined in our favor, but not without admonitions for our past failings. The pertinent part of the report read:

> After reviewing all the evidence, the Commission staff believes that no State purpose would be served if funds for the addition were delayed or denied, and that considerable damage to the educational program and the condition of the laboratory animals is quite likely in that event.
>
> Commission staff recommends that funds for the Life

Science Building Addition at UC Berkeley be approved.

This statement, plus the assurances of Chancellor Heyman to the legislators, carried the day. On May 20, 1984, the conference committee of both houses of the legislature met for a final time and, given the agreement reached with the university, approved funding for the first project of the biology reorganization. This agreement brought gloom to the animal rights activists; as well it might, for it was *the pivotal event* that turned the biology reorganization around from a project that I thought could never get off the ground into one that I could not have stopped if I had wanted to! We had turned the corner. Change was now inevitable.

In late May 1984, the contractor erected a fence behind the existing Life Sciences Building and started removing the trees and parking lot. The faculty realized that we were no longer talking about new biology facilities in the abstract. A new building was actually going to materialize; others would follow. How would each faculty member's programs be aided by these improvements? How would competition for grants, new graduate students, postdoctoral fellows, and faculty be affected? Whom did one want for neighbors and intellectual colleagues?

As a result of this event, there was a complete transformation from the climate of the Faculty Club discussion a few months earlier. The three coffin nails, faculty resistance, opposition by the legislative analyst, and the animal rights movement, were gone. What was originally a suspicious diffidence on the part of most faculty members became, overnight, a shameless scramble for position that subsequently led to the reduction of eleven separate departments into only three. Years of effort at planning and design could have been destroyed by a different outcome of the legislative hearings in the spring of 1984. A negative decision would also have destroyed the centerpiece of our highly successful capital campaign, as well as delaying modernization of the Berkeley biology program for many years. I'm glad, in retrospect, that our antagonists, the animal activists, didn't realize how much was at stake.

Our voyage from a conversation with the Koshlands at the Faculty Club to completion of the reorganization took almost twenty years. Its success involved hard work on the part of faculty leadership, political skill on the part of the chancellor, and acquisition of funds from loyal alumni, friends, and the legislature. More than one argument for doing something overcame the many arguments for resting on our laurels and doing nothing. Complacency, the parent of incompetence, fell before those who were young of heart and mind.

"We had a great adventure together."

– Daniel E. Koshland, Professor of Biochemistry at the University of California at Berkeley and former editor of the journal *Science* .

Chapter 11

Lesson 3 – Grade Inflation

Some Problems Are Not Worth Getting Bloody Over

What goes up doesn't always have to come down.
— New principle in social physics

During the 1960s, in parallel with the period of student unrest, an academic change was taking place in the classroom. The grades that students received for their work in the '60s and early '70s, particularly in the humanities and social sciences, were becoming higher. Over a ten-year period they rose from a C average to slightly greater than B. The loss in C grades was balanced by an increase in A's.

The reasons for this spontaneous change, which continues to this day, were an d still are unclear. Among the hypotheses offered by the media, faculty, and deans were:

- Introduction of evaluation of professors by students. It was postulated that professors gave higher grades to win popularity and promotion, on the premise that high grades are effective stimuli for favorable student evaluation and are also indicators of good teaching.

- A tendency among professors to compensate for marginal performance by poorly prepared nontraditional students. Awarding passing grades to weak students caused other students to move higher on the grading scale.

- Economic pressures on institutions. Lack of funds caused universities to try to retain all students as a source of additional income. The award of higher grades might be an incentive for a marginal student to stay enrolled.

- Colleges moving toward fewer required courses. Professors might compete for students in their classes by using higher grades as a marketing device.

- Belief by some professors that students should not experience failure. If students are positively reinforced regardless of their effort or performance, grade inflation results.

- A loss of confidence by faculty in their own values. An unsettling sense that Bob Dylan was correct: something was "blowin' in the wind," something professors did not understand, and therefore students were given the benefit of the doubt.

- A view that failure by a male student relegated him to possible death in an "immoral war" in Vietnam. To committed antiwar protesters, failing a student then became an immoral act.

The phenomenon of grade inflation was not limited to the Berkeley campus. It spread nationwide. Nowhere did higher average grades result from any deliberate change in academic policy. By the mid-1970s, grade inflation, if neglected by faculty members, had become a lively media topic, almost rivaling the media interest in "political correctness" today. A 1976 editorial in the *Wall Street Journal* pointed out that at Yale, 42% of all undergraduate grades in the previous spring term were A's, and 46% of the class graduated with honors. At Dartmouth in spring 1974, 41% of the senior grades were A's and 40% were B's. At Vassar, 81% of the undergraduate grades were A's and B's, and the same calculation at Amherst yielded 85%. The *Journal* noted further that Stanford had decided to reintroduce the D grade, but went on to observe that "such changes are still few in number. If the current easy grading, no grading ... and related systems continue, it may soon take a master's degree to qualify for a secretary's position."

The Los Angeles Times, in an editorial on August 22, 1976, stated bluntly:

> In grade schools no less than at the college level, student skills in reading, writing and mathematics have been declining steadily as measured by standard test results. At the same time student grade averages, based more on the subjective decisions of teachers, have been rising. Plainly, something is wrong here.

The *Times* writer was correct in that an important criterion for acceptance of an undergraduate into graduate school had become debased. Transcripts of a student's record were becoming increasingly meaningless with grade inflation. In addition, letters of recommendation were vaguer, damning only by faint praise, as students now had a right to see and challenge their letters of recommendation. The result was an increased dependence on standardized tests such as the GRE, LSAT, or MCAT to measure applicant quality.

As Dean of the College of Letters and Science at Berkeley, could I do anything to rectify these unplanned events and their consequences? I took the position that grade inflation at Berkeley, which was not the consequence of any conscious policy, should be reviewed by the College of Letters and Science's Executive Committee. My position immediately raised the interest of both the campus Academic Senate and the undergraduate student government. Approval of courses and grading policies at the University of California are delegated by the regents of the university to the faculty, and an inquiry by an administrator into grading practices could be viewed by many faculty members as interference, not only with a faculty prerogative but also with their academic freedom. The students, on the other hand, were divided. The more politically motivated students, for whom study was only a part-time activity, were satisfied with a trend that meant less work on their part to receive a high grade. They viewed any actions that would stimulate the Executive Committee to reverse this trend as a "take-away" that had not been discussed with the students. Of course, grade inflation, which had been going on for about eight years, had not been discussed with them or anyone else. Conversely, the best students were in favor of a grading system that would recognize them as excellent performers. If the average undergraduate GPA was 3.6 on a 0–4 scale, excellent students had little opportunity to demonstrate their abilities. In fact, inflated grading for them presented mainly a downside risk; poor performance on a single examination might pull them below the average GPA.

When confronting the faculty with uncomfortable facts, it is always preferable to have in hand strategies for dealing with them. I decided it would be impossible at Berkeley to develop a uniform grading policy for Letters and Sciences undergraduates. Such policies do exist in smaller schools with well-defined curricula, such as the Law School, but our faculty was simply too large and too diverse for any meaningful policy to emerge and be successfully implemented. We had to approach the problem through indirection.

It soon became apparent that the most effective way to address this sensitive academic issue was merely to disclose the grades and what they meant. The first proposal for such disclosure, initially made to me by Professor Joseph Tussman of Philosophy, and Professor Joseph Hodges of Statistics, was that every grade on a student's transcript would be accompanied by additional information indicating the meaning of that grade. They specifically recommended to me that each letter grade on an undergraduate student's transcript would be followed by the number of students in the course and the average grade given in that class. Alternatively, the number of students receiving that grade or better would be indicated. These two additional pieces of information would be followed by the usual unit and grade point designations.

This proposal eventually received approval from Academic Senate review committees, but the students had very mixed responses. The politically active element in the student body, as represented by the student government, was highly opposed to what they christened the "relative transcript" on the ground that it would increase competition and thus would weaken student solidarity and accompanying educational benefits. Their opposition was most succinctly expressed in a widely circulated flyer that asked, "What is the difference between Idi Amin and Dean Park?" and answered, "Relative transcripts!" The most academically able students liked the proposal. If they could now discover the most difficult courses and sections, they would be able to differentiate themselves from average students in the grades they received. It was not lost on us that, under these circumstances, the professors with conservative grading curves would begin to acquire more than their share of the best students.

Would students waste time by searching via word of mouth for the easy and hard courses? This question led to a second proposal, which emerged from my conversations with the ASUC and the Student Consulting Group of the College of Letters and Science. The ASUC asked to meet with me on the topic of grade inflation, to convince me that it was not a problem and that I should drop the issue. I agreed to the meeting, listened patiently to their arguments for about fifteen minutes, and then offered my second strategy. I said, "Each of you probably wastes a great deal of time talking with your friends about the quality and grading of multi-sectioned courses. Wouldn't it be helpful to you if we placed an entire record of grade distributions given in all undergraduate courses and sections in the library for each term, with only the instructor's name and no student names identified? Then you would be able to find the easily and harshly graded courses with much less effort, and you would have more time to spend on the subject matter itself."

After a short caucus, they suggested that certain sections would be way over-subscribed were such information available. I replied that I would be willing to assign the Greek Theatre to a course if the size of the lecture hall was the only consideration. The ASUC officers then argued that it was probably illegal to reveal grade information because it could, in a very small course, indicate personally protected information about a specific student. To their various concerns about disclosing grading practices by section and about relative transcripts I replied, "I don't understand your policy shift. When issues involve the institution rather than yourselves, you are always in favor of disclosure!" Perhaps, as stated earlier, what is true about faculty is also true of students. When it comes to other people's problems and money, they are extreme liberals. When it comes to their own, they are extreme conservatives.

By 1977, grading reports were made available in campus libraries, and the relative transcript proposal was placed on hold pending required changes in campus computing formats. The distribution of grade reports in the library continued through 1980 when I left the deanship to become vice chancellor at Berkeley. My successors did not continue the practice. The relative transcript was never introduced; it slowly suffocated under Academic Senate review and administrative malaise.* Meanwhile, except for a slight dip in average under-graduate GPA during 1984 – 85, which marked the switch from the quarter to the semester calendar, undergraduate GPA has remained constant at 3.0 plus or minus 0.02. The great grade inflation of 1960 – 1974 established a new benchmark for aver-age student performance at universities throughout the United States. No longer is it an issue — grade inflation is now only an historic bit of academic dust carefully swept under the fac-ulty rug.

---

* The Young Man in a Hurry is a narrow-minded and ridiculously youthful prig, who is inexperienced enough to imagine that something might be done before very long, and even to suggest definite things.... He may be known by his propensity to organize societies for the purpose of making silk purses out of sow's ears. This tendency is not so dangerous as it might seem; for it may be observed that the sows, after taking their washing with a grunt or two, trundle back unharmed to the wallow; and the purse market is quoted as firm. — F. M. Cornford

Chapter 12

Lesson 4 – Ethnic Studies

Some Problems Are Worth Getting Bloody Over

In 1969, for a second time, I voted in favor of an action by the Academic Senate, naively assuming I would not bear responsibility for the ensuing challenges. I voted with a majority to establish a Department of Ethnic Studies, an action I knew would burden others, but I could not imagine then that I would inherit the birth pains of this program in 1972.

In 1969 a coalition of students, faculty, and others who had been arguing for establishment of a Third World College was able to mount a Third World Strike of students and teaching assistants that proved effective in bringing many university functions to a halt. While the Third World College itself was never approved, a number of motivations led to approval of an Ethnic Studies Department at the Academic Senate meeting in spring 1969. Some professors believed that the subject matter of the proposed department had academic justification and that it would enrich the academic plurality of subjects studied at Berkeley. Though they remained skeptical about the academic merits of the proposed department, they saw it as a way to "buy off the trouble" of the Third World Strike as well as the constant agitation for a Third World College. A small minority saw the department as a means for diverting university resources to a useful sort of social engineering. The smallest minority of all saw the proposed department, and an alliance with the "community," as a ministry for radicalization of the campus and as a center for Marxist thought. In opposition, some pragmatic faculty members were opposed to establishing the department under any circumstances, finding it academically unjustified and likely to remove financial resources from existing departments.

The strike that preceded the vote had worked in that it certainly gained the attention of the campus. A few days before the Academic Senate meeting, I arrived about fifteen minutes early for my 8:00 a.m. Biology 1 course to find a group of young Afro-Americans haranguing my class of 700 students, urging them to leave and join the rally in Sproul Plaza. They were firm in their belief that the present structure of the university was incapable of meeting the needs of minority students, and that university processes were too cumbersome and too fraught with political pitfalls to meet these needs. They did not realize that over half of my Biology 1 class consisted of premeds, hardly a radical group, and when I took a vote the students decided to stay. But that outcome was the exception and not the rule.

The administration wisely decided not to promote the concept of a Third World College, but instead to support a department that could, if it proved itself, eventually evolve into a college. Twenty-four faculty positions were removed from the campus's uncommitted pool of faculty positions and assigned to the new Ethnic Studies Department, which had no faculty, no students, no curriculum, and no chair. Roger Heyns, the chancellor at that time, recruited Carl Mack, a respected Black educator, to head up the new department and put him to work recruiting faculty, staff, and administrators. The faculty positions were divided among the four competing ethnic groups—not surprisingly, in proportion to their relative political strengths. The Afro-Americans got 12 of the 24 positions, the Asian Americans received five, the Chicanos got four, and the Native Americans received three. Each of the four programs was to recruit a coordinator, who in turn would recruit faculty members. The first courses would be offered in fall 1969.

The first three years of this department's existence were not auspicious. The coordinator retained for each program proceeded with faculty hires. Many of these teaching recruits would by necessity be temporary lecturers at first, but the campus optimistically anticipated that these temporary faculty members would soon be replaced by regular professorial faculty.

The coordinator of the Afro-American program, Ron Lewis, in streetwise fashion, divided his twelve positions among more than thirty part-time non-tenure-track faculty members. The other three ethnic studies programs also hired no assistant professors, only lecturers. The large part-time group of temporary non-tenure-track appointments in the Afro-American program took on many elements of a patronage system, and became known somewhat derisively as Ron's "Charlie Brown Squad." At this time, in summer 1972, I assumed my first major administrative post at Berkeley, as Provost and Dean of the College of Letters and Science, and as part of the package, somewhat to my dismay, I was given the administration of the Department of Ethnic Studies, which unlike other departments was not assigned to an existing college.

The first morning in my new post I noticed several invoices from Ethnic Studies on my desk that had not been processed by my predecessor. The first for several thousand dollars was for services provided by the Rainbow Sign Restaurant to Afro-American Studies. This sum was ostensibly for a community cultural outreach program, but a good portion of it was for a performance by Sun Ra and his "Arkestra" of jazz musicians. My informants suggested that some of the funds found their way back to the people who had requested the services. A second invoice was for several hundred pounds of buffalo meat served by the Native American program at an intertribal meeting at an Oakland hotel. These questionable invoices were soon followed by enormous telephone bills, bills for use of university automobiles to travel to the Midwest, bills for T-shirts for community baseball teams, and bills for computers and an extensive array of playground equipment for a child-care center.

Just before I was placed in charge of the Ethnic Studies program, Ron Lewis had been "let go" by the administration. Lewis was on a one-year contract, and that contract, with concurrence of Chancellor Albert Bowker, was not renewed by my predecessor, English professor Jack Raleigh. Of course this action was seen by the community for what it actually was, a "firing," not a failure to rehire. Although Ron Lewis was no longer with the program, his Charlie Brown Squad remained for an additional year.

I needed a replacement coordinator. The questions for me became: Could I identify anyone within the Afro-American program who would help me rescue it? Could I neutralize the squad whose yearly contracts were threatened by increasing the academic standard of the programs? I was an outsider, I was white and male, I had a Ph.D. and a home in suburbia. I was not to be trusted.

I soon learned that the language currency of the less responsible among the Afro-American lecturers was quite foreign to university communication. It was the language of threat and intimidation. My instinctive reaction was correct; I must use the same language to be effective. There was no broader audience in the department that espoused traditional university discourse. It occurred to me that the best way to neutralize the situation for the remainder of the academic year, when the lecturer contracts terminated, was to start a formal inquiry into the department's financial transactions. This would encourage the squad to "lie low" during the review while they were not aware of what I actually knew. I met with internal auditors and asked them to look into long weekend automobile rentals that put 2,000 miles on a car, and into what seemed to be community use of the telephone. I met with the head of our Equipment Inventory Department and asked him to start looking for office equipment, sports equipment, playground equipment, and other items that were purchased over the past three years, as I had on good authority that some of it had been stolen or put to private use. But I had a further instruction. I said, "I don't want a final report. I want you to spend the remainder of the year doing follow-ups and asking still more questions until we get through next June." My guess was right. When the adventurers in the department knew I was looking, but didn't know how much I knew, they assumed a low profile.

My immediate challenge was to identify a new coordinator—a leader, someone with respectable academic credentials and with commitment to the purposes of the institution, who could start building the credibility of the program. This person would also have to stand political heat from those beneficiaries of Ron Lewis's patronage who would not be continued. Only one of some forty people in academic positions employed by Afro-American Studies during that first year moved to a tenure-track faculty title. Bil Banks, initially hired as a lecturer, had petitioned Ron Lewis for this transfer, which would place him on a tenure track with all the protections afforded by the Privilege and Tenure Committee of the Academic Senate. Ron Lewis saw this transfer as an advantage to the Afro-American Program because Bil could then serve on the Academic Senate Committee on Courses, which had to approve the Afro-American program offerings. Bil saw this transfer as a protection against some of the instability of the program administration. Several months after his transfer to assistant-professor status, Bil received a letter from Ron Lewis announcing that his services as assistant professor were no longer needed and he was relieved of his academic appointment! The Committee on Privilege and Tenure came to Bil's rescue, and, as of June 30, 1972, it was Ron Lewis who left the campus while Bil remained.

Bil was an excellent choice for coordinator. He had a future at Berkeley, he was committed to improving the department so that it could serve the Afro-American community in the research and teaching currency of Berkeley, and he had the calmness and strength to withstand the verbal attacks and physical threats that were certain to occur. The following September only two or three squad members were rehired.

As I look back on the ensuing years, a major struggle within the Ethnic Studies programs was defining the relationship of their programs to the "community." The first program to face the issue squarely was the Afro-American program under the leadership of Bil Banks. During his first year as coordinator, Bil concluded that he could not develop his program within the present agenda of the Ethnic Studies Department, which at that time was highly politicized and unified by a radical desire for their own turf. He started working with the well-developed Black community in the East Bay to convince them that his program could not hire the scholars of distinction that he wanted to recruit if his program remained in Ethnic Studies. He also convinced them that Afro-American Studies should be transferred to the College of Letters and Science as a department if it was to develop into an academic program in which the community could take pride. This move, much to the distress of the other three ethnic studies programs, was made on July 1, 1973. The transfer had a salutary impact on Ethnic Studies. Movement of the Afro-American program to the College of Letters and Science not only removed half the department's faculty positions, it also removed a great deal of political influence as well, and all but assured that a Third World College was unlikely to emerge. As regular faculty began to appear in the programs, they stabilized, but often at great cost to the junior faculty who had to reassert control over the programs and budgets that had yielded in some cases to excessive community control. The Asian American program was a particular victim of external influence, as it had encouraged community input into academic and financial decision making, and had become increasingly dominated by members of the radical League of Revolutionary Struggle (LRS) during the 1980s. Although LRS participation was defended by the more radical students, this influence was eventually removed by the regular faculty who reassumed program control.

The mutual distrust principle played out in many ways. A memorable event was a meeting called by the "community" (students, non-students, lecturers, and community people) to discuss the "issues" in a large hall in the student union. I arrived to find the makings of a trial court. The room was overflowing with more than 200 people. It exuded distrust at best and hostility at worst. Feeling outnumbered and knowing this assembly wanted to test my physical and emotional endurance rather than to obtain any information, I braced for the first question. "Provost Park, what are your qualifications, if any, to make any determinations whatsoever about a program in ethnic studies?" I answered, "I know very little about ethnic studies, and the curriculum is not determined by me. It is determined by the faculty and our Academic Senate. But I do know many minority citizens of California who are very concerned for the success of this program. I am certainly willing to invite them here to review our program and to advise us on any changes or improvements that should be made." And so it went for three hours. By the end, I was getting tired but dared not reveal my fatigue to the audience. When hunger finally called, we filed out of the room. I was accosted by a reporter for the nominally student newspaper. "What did you decide about the issues?" she asked. "Nothing," I replied. "These are issues we will work on for the next twenty years. There are no simple solutions to complex problems." This was not what the young radical wanted to hear, but distrust based on years of reinforcement cannot be erased in one afternoon.

Administering budgets and personnel actions as a young scientist did not train me to deal with the street politics of an ethnic studies program teetering on the fine edge of control. I believe the capacity to deal with these challenges is more the result of a deep sense of the human passion and motivation emanating from an audience than it is the result of any specific administrative training program. While technical skills can always be sharpened, intuition about organizing and directing people in a collegial environment may be based more on an innate sense about other human beings and expectations of them than on cookbook recipes.

In 2007, the ethnic studies program at Berkeley consisted of an established department reporting directly to the executive vice chancellor, with its own Ph.D. program and a participating Department of Afro-American Studies in the College of Letters and Science. This program is generally regarded as a leader among ethnic studies programs in the United States, and there is little to remind us of the department's turbulent beginnings thirty-seven years ago except in the memories of those of us who were present at its birth.

I have always projected that in twenty or thirty years Ethnic Studies, though it may remain as a group major, will not be needed as an academic department. The Ethnic Studies Department is a reaction to lack of such studies and faculty with these interests in the traditional departments. As the traditional departments become more successful in training and hiring a diverse faculty representing interests expressed in Ethnic Studies, the need for Ethnic Studies as a separate unit will lessen. In this sense, the long-term success of the Ethnic Studies Department may be measured by its own demise.

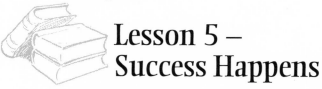

Chapter 13

Lesson 5 – Success Happens
The Bay Area Writing Project

> *What's wrong with it? There is nothing*
> *wrong with it. It is just no good!*
> — Carl Selle, English teacher,
> criticizing an RBP composition in 1948.

Once I became Provost and Dean of the College of Letters and Science in 1972, I discovered a perennial truth: Money is always in short supply. Additional state funds are generally designated for new academic "improvements," while bread-and-butter programs continue financially squeezed. This problem is particularly acute in public universities, in which money "comes in colors," having been designated by the legislature for specific programs. While funding of improvements appears socially progressive, the legislature at the same time designates an increased salary savings target for the university, which effectively designates a cut in other programs to pay for the "improvements." Consequently, the university, despite its designation as constitutionally immune, can be micromanaged by Sacramento through the budget process. The result is that I was on constant lookout for efficiencies and savings that could be used to reinforce core academic programs.

One possible source of such funds at Berkeley was the Subject A course, a remedial English program that had been in existence since 1898. There used to be three such programs: Subject A in remedial English; Subject B in remedial Latin; and Subject C in remedial high school mathematics. Subject B disappeared before the Second World War. Subject C persisted through the early 1960s when I first advised Berkeley students. In 1972, unless new freshmen exceeded a minimum score on the verbal SAT or passed an examination in Subject A, they were required to take this course. It constituted four units of work, but students received only two units of credit because of its remedial nature. In addition, students had to pay $40 for registering in the course, whether they passed it or not. The course, taught by lecturers and teaching assistants, actually cost the campus considerably more than $40 per student. It, of course, occurred to me that if more of our students placed out of Subject A, the course would become smaller, we would hire fewer temporary faculty members to teach it, and the funds saved could be diverted to freshman Reading and Composition. In fall, 1973, 41 percent of our new freshman class, or well over 1,000 students, had been enrolled in Subject A. Could this number be reduced?

There was, and still is, another reason for reducing enrollment in remedial English. The legislators concluded that if anyone paid for remedial English, it should be the high schools who failed to adequately prepare their graduates to do college-level work. Therefore, in 1973, the state calculated the previous year's cost of Subject A, and removed these funds from the base budget of the university. The university continued funding Subject A, and, in the early 1980s, the funds for Subject A were removed again.

If instant correction of the problem was an impossibility, particularly with increasing numbers of first-generation undergraduates, better elementary and secondary school preparation of college-bound seniors was possible. The question was how to encourage enthusiasm in secondary and elementary school English teachers about their subjects. Teachers as a group had become rightfully leery about university plans to make them more effective. In the early 1970s, "Why Johnny can't write" stories began to appear in the media, along with accounts of declining SAT scores by high school students. These teachers had endured many years of presidents of prestigious research universities "viewing with alarm" the decline in preparation of students graduating from high school, with no recognition of high schools' shrinking budgets and increased burdens.

Obviously, "viewing with alarm" the efforts of dedicated secondary-level teachers was not only an ineffective strategy for improvement, it was incorrect in its premise. University and school-level teachers had a shared problem of deficiencies in student literacy, critical thinking, and articulate expression. In my view, these problems run much deeper in our society than any mere deficiency in secondary or collegiate education. These skills in students are closely related to their intellectual values, which suffer from passive acceptance of television dialogue and dramatic plots in which problems are solved by "Ugh, Yes, No" utterances and violence rather than articulate expression. If we at the university had a shared problem with the schools, at least we could work on it together. On this premise, Supervisor of Teacher Education James Gray and I established a summer institute in 1974 that was to become the Bay Area Writing Project, the parent of the National Writing Project and grandparent of its international offspring.

After developing this strategy with my budget officer, Edward Feder, I approached Chancellor Albert Bowker for financial support. Al Bowker had served for a number of years as the head of the City University of New York, and had a deep understanding of the political nature of the world. He listened somewhat skeptically to my proposal for a $13,000 summer institute for twenty-five high school teachers of English. They would come to Berkeley for four weeks as College of Letters and Science fellows to work with our faculty on effective ways to improve student composition. We also intended to improve the teaching of critical thinking and articulate expression, which might lead to effective composition. Each teacher would receive a $500 stipend for the five-week institute, and $500 would cover the cost of a meeting at the Faculty Club for school administrators. We also envisioned that the fellows would work during the school year with other English teachers to improve their classes. I argued that the new approach would be successful because we were telling the teachers that they were important and that we needed their assistance. Al Bowker decided to support me, probably as a personal gesture, because I don't think he believed the summer program would have any impact on the problem I proposed to address, or that it would be of particular political value. Others agreed with him. The Berkeley public information officer at the time told me there was no use in putting out a press release on the program, because it was not news.

Once the funds were assured, I chose James Gray to assume the actual day-to-day administration of the institute. Jim Gray and Assistant Dean Bill Brandt of the Rhetoric Department, independently, had been developing their own plan for a summer writing institute for teachers of writing. They already knew many Bay Area English teachers, and had a good sense of those who were successful in their teaching efforts and who could provide leadership as teacher consultants to other teachers during the intervals between summer institutes. The teachers, from elementary through community college levels, were selected on the basis of interviews.

I attended the first meeting of the summer institute in June 1974. As I entered the room, I could sense latent suspicion among the teachers. They were obviously wondering *what kind of trip is this forty-two-year-old dean going to lay on us?* and were prepared for the worst. Before I spoke, Keith Caldwell, a teacher who was later to become a co-director of the institute, made an observation. "You've got a problem? Well, solve it yourself. We've got our own problems to worry about!" These were experienced, expert teachers with chips on their shoulders, ready to react to any hint of criticism or condescension. They were increasingly cynical of most school staff-development efforts with "tripod talks" by "take the money and run" consultants who in many cases had never taught in the schools. Worse yet, they had been required to attend such sessions. They were not looking to the university for imposed leadership or a cheerleading session.

I then addressed my wary audience. "Thank you for coming. You are important to us because we share an educational problem that neither of us can solve alone. It is the diminishing ability of our young people to write in a clear, articulate, and critical fashion. I'm not talking about creative writing. It is not our objective to produce Ernest Hemingways. I would be quite happy if students could look out that window (which happened to overlook the Hearst Mining Building) for a minute or so and could return to write a coherent paragraph about what they saw. To do so effectively, they would have to draw on their knowledge about the university, about the Hearsts, about architecture, and the role of aesthetics in human life. Most of them would not be able to do this initially, but if we are successful, they will strive for this ability. We can all write better with coaching, no matter what stage we are at. Professional athletes have coaches during their entire careers without embarrassment; why not writers also? The faculty members in this course will work with you as we look for effective methods in reaching students. It is my hope that as College of Letters and Science fellows you will become ambassadors for what we have learned and carry it to schools throughout the Bay Area."

Jim Gray and I had done something new. We were not treating the teachers in a "top down" fashion, a trademark of how universities traditionally regarded high school teachers within the academic pecking order. We had, instead, treated them as colleagues and professionals who would work in a pragmatic way to address a major educational challenge. An assumption of the institute, which proved correct, was that almost none of the teachers were trained to teach writing when they began their teaching careers. Instead, the elementary teachers had been trained to teach reading, and the secondary and college teachers had studied the history of English literature. Writing, so fundamental to student thinking and intellectual discipline, was and still is neglected in the university curriculum, possibly because it is time consuming to teach and because so few people have the self-confidence to teach it well. The successful teachers of writing who participated in the first institute found that they could learn useful techniques from each other and were anxious to train colleagues. They knew that the impulse to design "the model writing curriculum" would certainly have been premature and possibly too doctrinaire in the long run. Earlier efforts to produce "teacher-proof" materials, such as the excellent writing materials published by Project English in the mid-1960s, had almost no impact on the teaching of writing or student writing abilities. Our "bottom up" approach produced, over that summer of 1974, a set of enduring principles that would guide the institute and its offspring over the next thirty-two years, as it grew from twenty-five teachers to a national (the National Writing Project) and international program with over \$10 million per year in total support and more than 700,000 teachers participating.

The principles were:

1. All teachers of writing, kindergarten through university, belong to a single, interdependent, collegial community with shared professional challenges—challenges that will best be met through collaborative efforts based on mutual professional respect.

2. Teachers of writing must write; their authority as teachers of writing must be grounded in their own personal experience as writers as persons who know firsthand the struggles and satisfactions of the writer's task.

3. Classroom teachers (not visiting university specialists) are the most trustworthy and credible authorities on what works in classrooms, and the most effective in-service programs will be those in which successful classroom teachers share and pool their experience with colleagues through "hands-on" demonstration lessons.

4. A successful staff development program requires ongoing and continually renewed collaboration of teaching colleagues who will continue to share and pool their expertise beyond a few scheduled workshops or even beyond an extended summer institute.

5. What working teachers of writing know from their classroom experience constitutes valid professional knowledge, but as members of a profession, such teachers also need to challenge, validate, and enhance the authority of their experience by familiarizing themselves with recent developments in composition research and theory.

The Bay Area Writing Project expanded to California and then to all fifty states with 189 sites. In summer 1991, President George H. W. Bush signed a bill awarding $10 million to the National Writing Project to continue its work. Looking back on my participation at the birth of this highly successful core program in educational improvement, I have to ask, "Why did it work when so many other programs had failed?" Jim Gray tells me that my participation was timely and successful because I am a populist at heart. That is probably true, because I have always had little use for intellectual arrogance. Undoubtedly the most important element in the success of this grass-roots program was Jim's own skill as a teacher and inspirer of others.

Give strong teachers recognition and responsibility, and they will not only become more effective, they will also make you proud of what they accomplish. Despite the many problems universities faced during the past forty years, success happens!

Chapter 14

Leadership: The Rarest Commodity

Do I have the right stuff?

Question asked of former dean Lincoln Constance
by RBP in 1972 (see page 174).

As a new administrator, I assume your background is similar to that of most young academics, and that you are about to practice without a license. Since the task awaiting you is very sensitive to mistakes stemming from poor judgment or lack of experience, a few bits of advice can spare you some cuts, bruises, and stubbed toes. This short chapter summarizes my thoughts on developing qualities required by your new job.

What commodity in the world is in shortest supply? I sometimes asked my students this question. They answered, oil or perhaps steel or copper or electrical power. I responded, "You are all wrong. The world commodity in shortest supply is effective leadership coupled with a management team that can implement the leader's initiatives." Excellent leadership and management collectively constitute effective administration. Almost any enterprise of any size admits it could attain its goals better, often much better, with an improved administrative team. The improved team has many challenges, but a first priority is creation of a shared vision for their institution. This is another way

169

of saying the team will agree on strategic objectives. This vision will extend far beyond the ego needs of those in charge. The leader of this administrative team must incorporate this vision in all actions, and must translate this vision through staff and subordinates into effective action. To implement this vision, the new leader must possess the political skill to persuade members of the institution to follow, or if some remain not persuaded, to bypass those threatened by change who would prefer to follow the ruts in the road. Whether the enterprise is a department store, a school, a large industry, or a university, there is always room for administrative improvement.

When my students asked, "Why is this so difficult?" I responded, "Because administrators are human beings with all the potential and all the frailty that humans possess." An administration that demonstrates complementary strengths is the answer to this dilemma.

How does an academic institution become better led? Nothing will be improved very much until the "right" leader is in place.

Institutional searches for the right leader, the one who will create a vision and the team to implement it, are a continuous process. Of more than 3000 institutions of higher education in the United States, at any one time, more than 300 are looking for their next leader. This leader will solve their problems, will inspire them, and will make them willing and enthusiastic followers on an important institutional mission. The search for effective leaders has spawned a major industry as search firms spend full time finding the right person for the right job. How will the searchers know they have found the right person? At the core, some attributes of the right person who will inspire the institution and recruit an effective implementation team are universal.

The Right Person to Lead and Manage

About 1,600 new leadership and management books are published every year, each attempting to guide the reader toward more effective management styles. If effective administration is the goal of these books, and they truly reveal the path toward this goal, then why must three or four new books be published every day, year after year? Each volume presents its views defining leaders. Here follows my own definition.

1. Leaders know themselves. They have established their values through broad experience. Experience means that this person has faced a wide range of administrative challenges, has learned from them, and has emerged wiser and more skillful. Not only success, but occasional failures are necessary components of experience as they instruct, temper, and improve the skill of the leadership candidate.

2. Leaders have confidence in their values, and express them in all their actions. In this they are consistent and predictable. These values encompass a common good, and diminish the primate imperative for personal gain.

3. Leaders formulate and embody a vision for their institutions. An institution must know what it is and what it is trying to do. This vision must be generated with intense involvement of immediate staff, boards, and employees if the vision is to permeate the operation of the organization. The leader's action must constantly demonstrate this vision in all actions. This vision-generation exercise must be repeated at regular intervals so that new staff, employees, and board members continue internalizing the vision for the organization.

4. Leaders who know themselves as others see them, staff

171

to their weaknesses. Leaders without self-knowledge and misplaced self-confidence hire people like themselves, and administrative weaknesses remain unaddressed. The best decisions result from debate among strong, intelligent participants. Selection of effective staff who can implement the leader's vision is essential for the institution's success. A vision without implementation is an empty rhetorical exercise.

5. Leaders develop policies that reward employees who demonstrate outstanding performance. They also guide employees who do not. This is essential for maintaining morale and implementing the leader's vision.

6. Leaders are equally transmitters and receivers of information as well as values. They effectively "read" their political environment, their associates, and those they interview for key positions in the organization. Reading is a task that can be honed and improved with experience, but it does not reside equally in all individuals. A five-minute personal interview following review of a curriculum vita can be very informative. How do applicants speak and present themselves? The experienced leader reads the person from the moment they enter the room, from the way they walk (are they confident and deliberate) to motions of their hands (are they nervous and uncertain) to their facial expressions and their eyes (are they presenting themselves honestly or are they acting out, not themselves, but who they think they should be?) How do they respond to a question such as "Why do you think you should have this job?" Are they thoughtful or too glib? The leader soon senses the substance of the job applicant, and may have a unique criterion such as one of my own: Would I take this person on a double-handed sailboat race from San Francisco to Japan? Would

this person become stronger in the face of challenges, or would the person, as difficulties mount, run below and pull a pillow over their head?

7. Leaders, when appearing before an audience, after a short time speaking and watching responses and listening to the background noise, begin to "read" the deepest hopes, aspirations, and fears of this audience. The leader then needs the oratorical skill and rhetorical power to persuade the assembled to join a proposed course of action. This is another way of saying leaders have equal numbers of "receivers" and "transmitters."

8. A leader develops an information grapevine in addition to the formal reporting structure. Staff members who share the leader's values will informally warn the leader of impending difficulty. The leader will know whether such communications are to be taken seriously depending on their source.

9. A true leader is called upon to make difficult decisions that may affect the livelihood of employees. This calls upon the humanity and political skill of the leader who will end up being loved by some and in all probability disliked by others. But the successful leader must always be seen as loyal to the values of the institution and working toward the common good, not toward self-interest. Such a leader will inspire employees to say, "We would follow you down the mouth of a cannon."

10. A good leader knows when it is time to step down. All administrators have a limited "political bank account" that, as they implement their decisions, sooner or later is empty. Then it is time for someone unscarred by past decisions to take the reins. Knowing that it is desirable to leave while some may still miss you, the true public

173

servant senses when this time approaches and formulates an exit strategy that is least disruptive to the institution. Part of this exit strategy is to develop potential successors. If they are developed too early they will become dissatisfied and leave for another institution. If they are developed too late, they will not be prepared to take the reins. Lesser leaders deceive themselves and attempt to endure beyond their effectiveness, usually much to the detriment of the institution.

My Journey to These Conclusions

When I was asked to become Dean of the College of Letters and Science at Berkeley thirty-seven years ago, I sought the advice of Professor Lincoln Constance, a former successful dean of the college. I asked him, "Do I have the right stuff?" His response was: "Academic leadership takes three attributes: the wisdom of Solomon, the patience of Job, and the stomach of a goat!" But then he went on to say: "If you do the 'people' part right, it does not matter too much what else you do that is wrong. But if you do the 'people' part wrong, it does not matter too much what else you do that is right." This advice proved sound. Equally applicable to management is what Chief Justice Potter Stewart said in 1984 about pornography in *Jacobellis vs. Ohio.* "Maybe I can't define it, but I know it when I see it!"

So it is with academic institutions. I think we all recognize some generic characteristics of the institution benefiting from strong leadership. In the well-led university, morale is high among students, staff, and faculty alike. The mission of the institution is defined, and is agreed upon which indicates that a successful political process has been in place. There is confidence in evenhanded fairness by the institution, from the award of grades to the students to the award of merit pay to faculty and staff. There is a belief that the institution is much more than any individual in it, and, from this combination of factors, loyalty results.

But how is this nirvana achieved? Our institutions have different histories, and we as individuals all have different strengths and weaknesses. Clearly, there is no prescribed road to paradise; rather, there are many strategies and administrative structures. My point is that leadership style must be adapted to institutional traditions and history so that the institution's values and goals are reinforced most effectively.

The variability among institutions is indicated in figure 1. First there is the traditional style, which we all know is not the way institutions really work. A former colleague of mine described this comforting chart as "the way the players line up before the ball is snapped!" The second style is the Council of Deans or Politburo style.

The third is the all bosses and no workers style, which characterizes many small radical organizations. The Symbionese Liberation Army comes to mind, in which all members seem to be field marshals! The fourth style I call the "end run by a one-issue group" style (typical of what many of us face from day to day in universities). The fifth is the ultimate decentralization style, and the sixth is the Dean of Letters and Science, or as it is described on the chart, "Chinese style." The one issue style has many variants reflected both locally and internationally. Now we come to the shared governance style exemplified by UC Berkeley or the University of Wisconsin! I suggest each of you enlarge this diagram for use the next time a faculty member complains that he or she was not consulted. Ask where he or she fits on this chart! Finally, we have the divine guidance or strong chancellor style, the Mafia style, and the Italian city state or Harvard "each tub on its own bottom style."

Figure 1: Some Organization Charts

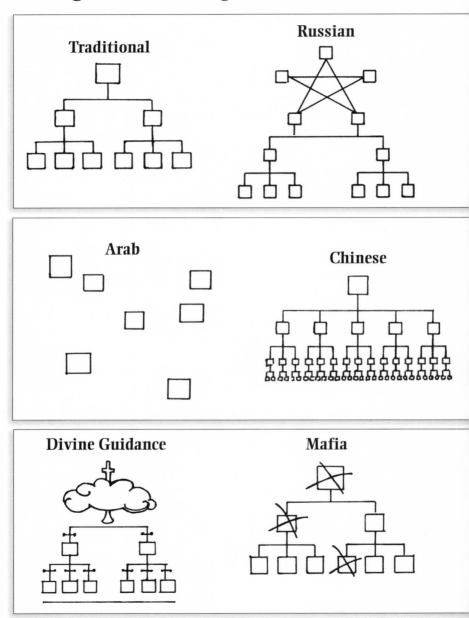

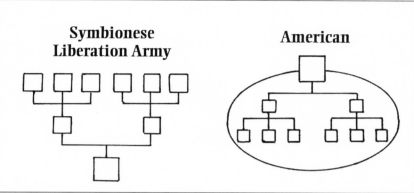

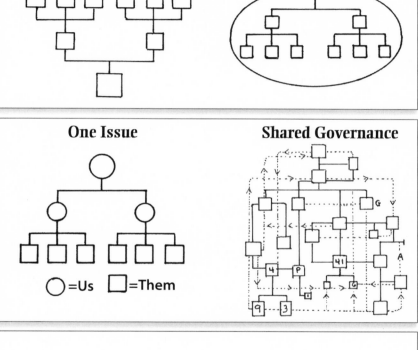

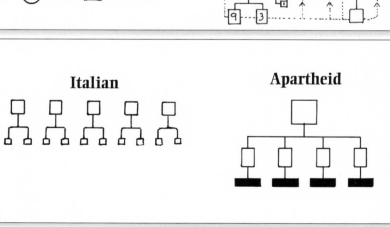

We can conclude from this potpourri that there is no prescriptive management style that will work for all institutions, particularly those with a collegial environment such as the university. The collegial environment is a very flat administrative structure, unlike the hierarchies of the army or the church, and is thus very easily perturbed. This means that it is harder to bring about changes in the collegial environment, and any leadership that is effective must recognize both the values and the goals of the institution and its dynamics.

In this sense, it is useful to look at the expectations of a chief academic officer to find what characteristics are needed in addition to the ten definitions given earlier. To begin with, the role of the chief academic officer has changed over the past thirty or forty years. It is my empirical observation that the chief academic officers are becoming more like the executive officer on a ship. They manage most of the day-to-day internal activities, and act for the captains when the captains are absent. I believe, along with Professor Martin Trow, that the chief academic officer should exhibit four leadership characteristics: symbolic, political, managerial, and academic.

Symbolic leadership is the ability of the chief academic officer to formulate, articulate, project, and even to embody the character of the institution and to present its values and goals in a forceful and inspiring way. I'm not sure this dimension can be successfully taught if a person lacks the passion and belief in the institution that are central to such leadership. Inside the university, it is this kind of leadership that explains and justifies the institution and its decisions to a campus community. It does this by linking the structure and process of the campus to the larger goals of teaching and learning in an environment of ever-increasing knowledge. Successfully done, such internal leadership strengthens the motivation and morale of the campus participants. Off campus, with alumni, the legislature, the press, and trustees or regents, the chief academic officer's ability to articulate the goals and values of the institution in a consistent way helps shape and convey its image. Such activity is vital for gaining financial and political support as well as for recruiting able faculty, staff, and students.

Political leadership refers to a chief academic officer's capacity to resolve the conflicting demands and pressures of various departments, colleges, faculty, student groups, and one-issue groups, both internal and external, in such a way that the institution's goals and purposes remain evident so that support can be gained for them. Political leadership, then, is a translation of symbolic imagery into the real world of competing demands and ambitions. The successful chief academic officer, while often saying no, and saying yes only occasionally, must constantly ask: "What makes the best sense for the institution ten years down the road?" and must emerge relatively unscathed from this challenge. I have often compared the chief academic officer to a wood piling driven into San Francisco Bay. At first it is new and shiny and shows none of the penalties of age. With increasing age, it will accumulate more barnacles and borers until there is little sense in fixing it. The time to drive a shiny new piling has arrived. If we are implementing real decisions to improve the institution, we cannot remain unscathed forever, no matter how careful we are.

Managerial leadership is, for most of us, the ability to direct and coordinate support activities of the institution in a way that is compatible with the institution's central goals and values. At the center of this managerial effort is the chief academic officer's ability to use perceptive judgment in the selection of staff. Whereas the CAO of a small college may undertake many managerial decisions without delegation, the CAO of a large and complex institution must be able to rely on the integrity of decisions of unit managers from various support activities. If we do a poor job in filling these positions, it does not really matter what other plans we develop, because they will not be properly implemented. We are all human beings with strengths and weaknesses; it is the successful leader who understands his or her strengths and weaknesses, and staffs to the weaknesses. I think we all know strong individuals who have surrounded themselves with somewhat weak, like-thinking supporters. Such institutions inevitably are weakened because the leader has not chosen individuals who complement the leader's strengths. Strong leadership and strong complementary support staff is one sign of a well-led institution.

The fourth component of leadership is academic; it shows itself over the long term and ultimately by the ability of the chief academic officer, through the deans and staff officers, to place in priority order the academic challenges facing the institution, so that the CAO knows where and how to intervene to strengthen academic structures. Resources are limited; we cannot say yes to everyone. When and where we say no is often a critically important decision. How we say it must be credible. Oscar Wilde's famous line, "not to decide is to decide," is also relevant in this process. Academic leadership shows itself in the ability to recognize excellence in teaching and research and in the choice of able deans and administrators who will be effective in the recruitment and advancement of talented teachers, scholars, and staff.

I have just described a paragon, a leader who understands and embodies the symbolic character of the institution and translates it to the public, who can maneuver this vision through day-to-day political challenges of internal and external groups, who understands effective management and maintenance of morale in the support staff, and who has the academic credibility and knowledge to set an agenda of priorities that is accepted by the faculty, students, staff, and alumni. No one has all of these characteristics in equal measure. The obvious importance of staffing to our weaknesses is apparent. Great leaders know their limitations, and they staff to promote their efforts. They are not afraid of strong people around them. Only weak leaders surround themselves with sycophants.

Beyond being a good manager and making good appointments, there are two principal components of leadership mentioned earlier. The first is obvious and well understood, the knowledge and political acumen to make the right decisions most of the time, to recognize when decisions are not correct, and to modify them and recover. There is a second part of decision making that is as important as, or even more important than, the first: the ability to legitimize the decisions made to the point that one has sufficient political support to govern.

There are, of course, many other "rules" of management, but so often they become technical and appear in manuals titled something like *Tilly's Typing Tips*. Can management be taught? A great many consultants, who are often failed managers themselves, believe that it can. The hiring of an "expert" to present a workshop or a "tripod talk" is a common strategy for in-service training of a management team. The expert, who often appears to be a recent graduate of Dale Carnegie, is at a disadvantage because such sessions rarely have the follow-ups necessary to maintain momentum. A particularly trying experience is the tripod talk in which the presenter places about twenty cards on a tripod and then proceeds, serially, to read them to the audience. Most audiences can already read, and become vaguely suspicious that the experts have such poor memories that they cannot do without their graphic props! Once through the session, the "expert" generally takes the check and is never seen again.

So much for useful leadership hints in an academic setting.

An Effective Alternative to the Tripod Talk: Dealing with Hostile Audiences

A refreshing change in the all too common tripod scenario was a public speaking course, taught at Berkeley, designed to help the participants deal with hostile audiences. Given the frequency with which Berkeley administrators address hostile groups, such skill development certainly could not harm us and might be of considerable use, so seven administrators signed up during the academic year 1989–90. The course was a set of ten sessions in which we would discuss briefly the points for the day and then give short speeches or prepared pieces on topics ranging from the campus long-range development plan to the handling of animal rights protests or actual interviews on surprise topics. Our talks and responses were recorded on video. These videos were subsequently criticized by the leader of the course, by expert interviewers brought in from local radio and television stations, or by our fellow students, and then we tried again.

Not all vice chancellors would be willing to expose themselves to such public exposure, criticism, and possible humiliation; however, the experience was not only rewarding, it also did something way beyond improving a skill. It allowed seven administrators to get to know and support each other at a level that could not be achieved by our usual interactions. We came to know about each others' childhoods, education, and "maturing experiences." We learned under fire from each other's mistakes and successes, and increased our skills by doing, not just discussing. Now, when we see a television interviewer asking a complicated question with a twist at the end—such as "Don't you think that is dishonest?"—we know the questioner is hoping that the subject of the interview will start the answer with "No, that is not dishonest," thus firmly planting the word "dishonest" in the viewer's mind. We know that once you hear the key word in the question, you start composing what you want to say about it regardless of the question. We know that you don't have to answer the question, but can change it into something else by a phrase such as "The real problem underlying (fill in key words here) is the larger issue of __."! We know that no matter how severe the attack from the audience, we will start our answer by some measure of agreement, even if only to say, "I suppose the issue could be viewed that way, but if we take into account..." We know that we don't look at our most severe critics during our answer; we look at the rest of the audience because they might be convinced, whereas the questioner has a mind made up.

We played roles. The person being tested sat at the center of the group while the others assumed the roles of specific regents questioning a specific issue. Humor had its place, and I recall the chancellor's assistant, John Cummins, being asked, after animal protesters had broken through campus police lines and resupplied colleagues who were sitting atop a construction crane for the new animal facility, "Who is your police chief, Mack Sennet?"

Skill development has its place, but it is not obtained from flashy brochures and cheerleading consultants who make their presentations and run. It is accomplished by managers meeting the consultant, and each other, halfway. It is learning from each other, and learning by doing with a coach.

Getting the Right People into the Right Jobs

If you don't have the right people in the right jobs, life can become impossible, or at least miserable. In this sense, universities are much like ocean-racing sailboats. No matter the weather or circumstances, you don't throw anyone overboard in the middle of the ocean; rather, you find jobs that best fit individual skills and competencies. Every effort is made to elicit from crew members a sense of contribution to the total racing effort. Small changes make enormous differences in the morale of the crew and thus in the speed of the sailboat. This is illustrated by asking a question: "What's the difference between heaven and hell?" The answer is that the people in heaven and hell are all about the same. They are working hard and trying to do a good job; however, different people are doing different jobs. In heaven the French are chefs, the English are policemen, the Germans are technicians, the Swiss are administrators, and the Italians are lovers. But in hell, the English are chefs, the Germans are policemen, the French are technicians, the Swiss are lovers, and the Italians are administrators! This concludes my thoughts on how to lead and manage the unmanageable.

But there are also certain empirical rules that I have used to lighten stress and conflict when seemingly intractable conflicts arise. As players on the administrative stage, we often forget that we are engaged in reruns of old dramas. When seen as "theater of the absurd," these frustrations are often reduced to pathetic foibles of our human existence. Here are some of these empirical rules, which you may find useful and to which you should add your own.

1. Everything worth doing isn't worth *your* doing. This is the first rule of delegation.

2. Without structures to the contrary, work flows to the competent person until he or she collapses. This is the second rule of delegation.

3. It is easier to take a step in the right direction than to know exactly where you are going. This is the first rule of planning.

4. When alligators are nipping at your heels, it is difficult to remember that you are there to drain the swamp. This is the second rule of planning.

5. If you are going to leap a chasm, don't do it in two steps! This is the third rule of planning.

6. Budget reductions are not all bad. Every crisis is an opportunity. This is the fourth rule of planning.

7. Never underestimate the power of administrative delay. This is the final rule of planning.

8. Nothing is ever a complete failure; you can always use it as a bad example.

9. Be calm, collected, and not upset, because no matter what you do, somebody will give you one or more of the following responses: You are (a) wrong; (b) insensitive; (c) a bleeding heart; (d) a pawn of somebody else; (e) too wishy-washy; (f) too unwilling to compromise; (g) all of the above. Consistency is not required of critics!

10. The rule of information is that the information you want is not what you need; the information you need is not what you can obtain; the information that you can obtain costs more than you want to pay; your computing office will tell you that the agony of today is justified by the promise of tomorrow.

11. If you enjoy having people like you, fine, but if you need them to like you, get a dog. Name this rule after your dog.

12. In dealing with their own problems and money, faculty are extreme conservatives. In dealing with other people's problems and money, they are extreme liberals. This is the law of faculty self-righteousness.

13. In dealing with other people's problems and money, students are extreme liberals. In dealing with their own problems and money they are extreme conservatives. This is the law of student self-righteousness.

14. An important rule involves how you deal with the institutional attitude:

There is only one argument for doing something, and the rest are arguments for doing nothing.
— F. M. Cornford

Although you can't make a horse drink, it is possible to lead it to water. For faculty members, it is impossible even to lead them to water unless you are clever enough to make them think it is their idea.

15. A second version of this rule: there is no limit to what you can accomplish if you give someone else the credit.

16. The "power broker" rule: It is often easier to gain forgiveness than permission! A corollary to this rule is, if you don't want the answer, don't ask the question!

17. You will become known by your friends and your enemies. Be proud of both lists!

18. When negotiating, remember that trust and distrust are almost always mutually shared. Occasionally use empathy and wear your opponent's shoes.

19. Anything is possible if you don't know what you are talking about!

20. "The number of rogues is about equal to the number of men who act honestly; and it is very small."
—F.M.Cornford.

21. Age and treachery will always take the field against mere youth and skill!

22. In ancient times, leaders always traveled with a shaman and a bodyguard. The shaman ordained the future, and the bodyguard protected the leader from attack. Today's leaders travel with economists and lawyers for the same purposes.

23. To sustain programs over the long term, one cannot count on such ephemeral human emotions as love and goodwill. In the long run one must also appeal to the more basic emotions of greed or avarice.

24. When your solution is deficient but is the best you can provide, remember what the snowman said: "Snowballs are better than no balls at all."

25. In a similar vein: If you are going to keep your head in the sand, hang your hat on your backside!

26. Friends come and go, but enemies accumulate.

27. If you are uncertain about the propriety of an action, ask, "How will I explain this when it appears on the front page of the local paper?" (Because it will!)

28. "Fire all indispensable people immediately." — Harold Ross, first editor of *The New Yorker.*

29. As a manager/leader, you will eventually be used up. Many hard decisions will leave your administrative bank account empty. There comes a time to move on and pass the reins to a new driver. At this point you will have a list of friends and enemies; again (recall from #17) the important thing is be proud of both lists!

30. Remember, when some individual is frustrating beyond belief, that elimination of this person will not solve the problem, because if that person did not exist, that individual would have to be invented.

31. Long procedural requirements are like the compulsory figures in ice skating—they are often the ticket to more creative activities.

32. Never wrestle with a pig—the pig will enjoy it and you will only get dirty.

Effective leadership and management at the university require a deep sense of the passion and beliefs held by the many constituencies who want the university to be responsive to their desires and needs. A balancing of these interests in a secure atmosphere that both supports free inquiry and maintains heroic expectations for human accomplishment is the goal of university leadership and management. How well you achieve these goals depends mostly on your own values and judgments, which might be enhanced by artfully applying the principles of this chapter.

Appendix

Microcosmographia Academica

**Being a Guide for the
Young Academic Politician**

By F. M. Cornford

Advertisement

If you are young, do not read this book;
it is not fit for you;
If you are old, throw it away;
you have nothing to learn from it;
If you are unambitious, light a fire with it;
you do not need the guidance.

But, if you are neither less than twenty-five years old,
nor more than thirty;
And if you are ambitious withal,
and your spirit hankers after academic politics;
Read, and may your soul (if you have a soul) find mercy!

Warning

'Any one of us might say, that although in words he is not able to meet you at each step of the argument, he sees as a fact that academic persons, when they carry on study, not only in youth as a part of education, but as the pursuit of their maturer years, most of them become decidedly queer, not to say rotten; and that those who may be considered the best of them are made useless to the world by the very study which you extol.

> *'Well, do you think that those who say so are wrong?'*
> *'I cannot tell,' he replied; 'but I should like to know what is your opinion?'*
> *'Hear my answer; I am of opinion that they are quite right.'*
> — Plato, *Republic VI*

My heart is full of pity for you, O young academic politician. If you *will* be a politician you have a painful path to follow, even though it be a short one, before you settle down into a modest incompetence. While you are young you will be oppressed, and angry, and increasingly disagreeable. When you reach middle age, at five-and-thirty, you will become complacent and, in your turn, an oppressor; those whom you oppress will find you still disagreeable; and so will all the people whose toes you trod upon in youth. It will seem to you then that you grow wiser every day, as you learn more and more of the reasons why things should not be done, and understand more fully the peculiarities of powerful persons, which make it quixotic even to attempt them without first going through an amount of squaring and lobbying sufficient to sicken any but the most hardened soul. If you persist to the threshold of old age—your fiftieth year, let us say—you will be a powerful person yourself, with an accretion of peculiarities which other people will have to study in order to square you. The toes you will have trodden on by this time will be as the sands on the seashore; and from far below you will mount the roar of a ruthless multitude of young men in a hurry. You may perhaps grow to be aware what they are in a hurry to do. They are in a hurry to get you out of the way.

O young academic politician, my heart is full of pity for you now; but when you are old, if you will stand in the way, there will be no more pity for you than you deserve; and that will be none at all.

I shall take it that you are in the first flush of ambition, and just beginning to make yourself disagreeable. You think (do you not?) that you have only to state a reasonable case, and people must listen to reason and act upon it at once. It is just this conviction that makes you so unpleasant. There is little hope of dissuading you; but has it occurred to you that nothing is ever done until every one is convinced that it ought to be done, and has been convinced for so long that it is now time to do something else? And are you not aware that conviction has never yet been produced by an appeal to reason, which only makes people uncomfortable? If you want to move them, you must address your arguments to prejudice and the political motive, which I will presently describe. I should hesitate to write down so elementary a principle, if I were not sure you need to be told it. And you will not believe me, because you think your cases are so much more reasonable than mine can have been, and you are ashamed to study men's weaknesses and prejudices. You would rather batter away at the Shield of Faith than spy out the joints in the harness.

I like you the better for your illusions; but it cannot be denied that they prevent you from being effective, and if you do not become effective before you cease to want anything to be done—why, what will be the good of you? So I present you with this academic microcosmography—the merest sketch of the little world that lies before you. A satirist or an embittered man might have used darker colours; and I own that I have only drawn those aspects which it is most useful that you, as a politician, should know. There is another world within this microcosm—a silent, reasonable world, which you are now bent on leaving. Some day you may go back to it; and you will enjoy its calm the more for your excursion in the world of unreason.

Now listen, and I will tell you what this outer world is like.

II. Parties

First, perhaps, I had better describe the parties in academic politics; it is not easy to distinguish them precisely. There are five; and they are called Conservative Liberals, Liberal Conservatives, Non-placets, Adullamites, and Young Men in a Hurry.

A *Conservative Liberal* is a broad-minded man, who thinks that something ought to be done, only not anything that anyone now desires, but something which was not done in 1881–82.

A *Liberal Conservative* is a broad-minded man, who thinks that something ought to be done, only not anything that anyone now desires; and that most things which were done in 1881–82 ought to be undone.

The men of both of these parties are alike in being open to conviction; but so many convictions have already got inside, that it is very difficult to find the openings. They dwell in the Valley of Indecision.

The *Non-placet* differs in not being open to conviction; he is a man of principle. A principle is a rule of inaction, which states a valid general reason for not doing in any particular case what, to unprincipled instinct, would appear to be right. The Non-placet believes that it is always well to be on the Safe Side, which can be easily located as the northern side of the interior of the Senate House. He will be a person whom you have never seen before, and will never see again anywhere but in his favourite station on the left of the place of judgment.

The *Adullamites* are dangerous, because they know what they want; and that is, all the money there is going. They inhabit a series of caves near Downing Street. They say to one another, 'If you will scratch my back, I will scratch yours; and if you won't, I will scratch your face.' It will be seen that these cave-dwellers are not refined, like classical men. That is why they succeed in getting all the money there is going.

The *Young Man in a Hurry* is a narrow-minded and ridiculously youthful prig, who is inexperienced enough to imagine that something might be done before very long, and even to suggest definite things. His most dangerous defect being want of experience, everything should be done to prevent him from taking any part in affairs. He may be known by his propensity to organise societies for the purpose of making silk purses out of sows' ears. This tendency is not so dangerous as it might seem; for it may be observed that the sows, after taking their washing with a grunt or two, trundle back unharmed to the wallow; and the purse-market is quoted as firm. The Young Man in a Hurry is afflicted with a conscience, which is apt to break out, like measles, in patches. To listen to him, you would think that he united the virtues of a Brutus to the passion for lost causes of a Cato; he has not learnt that most of his causes are lost by letting the Cato out of the bag, instead of tying him up firmly and sitting on him, as experienced people do.

O young academic politician, know thyself!

III. Caucuses

A Caucus is like a mouse-trap; when you are outside you want to get in; and when you are inside the mere sight of the other mice makes you want to get out. The trap is baited with muffins and cigars—except in the case of the Non-placet caucus, an ascetic body, which, as will presently be seen, satisfies only spiritual needs.

The *Adullamites* hold a Caucus from time to time to conspire against the College System. They wear blue spectacles and false beards, and say the most awful things to one another. There are two ways of dispersing these anarchs. One is to suggest that working hours might be lengthened. The other is to convert the provider of muffins and cigars to Conservative Liberalism. To mention belling the cat would be simply indecent.

No one can tell the difference between a *Liberal Conservative* Caucus and a *Conservative Liberal* one. There is nothing in the world more innocent than either. The most dare-devil action they ever take is to move for the appointment of a Syndicate 'to consider what means, if any, can be discovered to prevent the Public Washing of Linen, and to report, if they can see straight, to the Non-placets.' The result is the formation of an invertebrate body, which sits for two years, with growing discomfort, on the clothes-basket containing the linen. When the Syndicate is so stupefied that it has quite forgotten what it is sitting on, it issues three minority reports, of enormous bulk, on some different subject. The reports are referred by the Council to the Non-placets, and by the Non-placets to the wastepaper basket. This is called 'reforming the University from within.'

At election time each of these two Caucuses meets to select for nomination those members of its own party who are most likely to be mistaken by the Non-placets for members of the other party. The best results are achieved when the nominees get mixed up in such a way that the acutest of Non-placets cannot divine which ticket represents which party. The system secures that the balance of power shall be most happily maintained, and that all the Young Men in a Hurry shall be excluded.

The *Young Men in a Hurry* have no regular Caucus. They meet, by twos and threes, in desolate places, and gnash their teeth.

The *Non-placet* Caucus exists for the purpose of distributing Church patronage among those of its members who have adhered immovably to the principles of the party.

All Caucuses have the following rule. At Caucus meetings which are only attended by one member (owing to that member's having omitted to summon the others), the said member shall be deemed to constitute a quorum, and may vote the meeting full powers to go on the square without further ceremony.

IV. On Acquiring Influence

Now that you know about the parties and the Caucuses, your first business will be to acquire influence. Political influence may be acquired in exactly the same way as the gout; indeed, the two ends ought to be pursued concurrently. The method is to sit tight and drink port wine. You will thus gain the reputation of being a good fellow; and not a few wild oats will be condoned in one who is sound at heart, if not at the lower extremities.

Or, perhaps, you may prefer to qualify as a *Good Business Man.*

He is one whose mind has not been warped and narrowed by merely intellectual interests, and who, at the same time, has not those odious pushing qualities which are unhappily required for making a figure in business anywhere else. He has had his finger on the pulse of the Great World—a distant and rather terrifying region, which it is very necessary to keep in touch with, though it must not be allowed on any account to touch you. Difficult as it seems, this relation is successfully maintained by sending young men to the Bar with Fellowships of £200 a year and no duties. Life at the Bar, in these conditions, is very pleasant; and only good business men are likely to return. All business men are good; and it is understood that they let who will be clever, provided he be not clever at their expense.

V. The Principles of Government, of Discipline (Including Religion), and of Sound Learning

These principles are all deducible from the fundamental maxim, that the first necessity for a body of men engaged in the pursuit of learning is freedom from the burden of political cares. It is impossible to enjoy the contemplation of truth if one is vexed and distracted by the sense of responsibility. Hence the wisdom of our ancestors devised a form of academic polity

in which this sense is, so far as human imperfection will allow, reduced to the lowest degree. By vesting the sovereign authority in the Non-placets (technically known as the 'Senate' on account of the high average of their age), our forefathers secured that the final decision should rest with a body which, being scattered in country parsonages, has no corporate feeling whatever, and, being necessarily ignorant of the decisive considerations in almost all the business submitted to it, cannot have the sense of any responsibility, except it be the highest, when the Church is in danger. In the smaller bodies, called 'Boards,' we have succeeded only in minimizing the dangerous feeling, by the means of never allowing anyone to act without first consulting at least twenty other people who are accustomed to regard him with well-founded suspicion. Other democracies have reached this pitch of excellence; but the academic democracy is superior in having no organised parties. We thus avoid all the responsibilities of party leadership (there are leaders, but no one follows them), and the degradations of party compromise. It is clear, moreover, that twenty independent persons, each of whom has a different reason for not doing a certain thing, and no one of whom will compromise with any other, constitute a most effective check upon the rashness of individuals.

I forgot to mention that there is also a body called the 'Council', which consists of men who are firmly convinced that they are business-like. There is no doubt that some of them are Good Business Men.

The principle of Discipline (including Religion) is that *'there must be some rules.'* If you inquire the reason, you will find that the object of rules is to relieve the younger men of the burdensome feeling of moral or religious obligation. If their energies are to be left unimpaired for the pursuit of athletics, it is clearly necessary to protect them against the weakness of their own characters. They must never be troubled with having to think whether this or that ought to be done or not; it should be

settled by rules. The most valuable rules are those which ordain attendance at lectures and at religious worship. If these were not enforced, young men would begin too early to take learning and religion seriously; and that is well known to be bad form. Plainly, the more rules you can invent, the less need there will be to waste time over fruitless puzzling about right and wrong. The best sort of rules are those which prohibit important, but perfectly innocent, actions, such as smoking in College Courts, or walking to Madingley on Sunday without academical dress. The merit of such regulations is that, having nothing to do with right or wrong, they help to obscure these troublesome considerations in other cases and to relieve the mind of all sense of obligation towards society.

The Roman sword would never have conquered the world if the grand fabric of Roman Law had not been elaborated to save the man behind the sword from having to think for himself. In the same way the British Empire is the outcome of College and School discipline and of the Church Catechism.

The Principle of Sound Learning is that the noise of vulgar fame should never trouble the cloistered calm of academic existence. Hence, learning is called sound when no one has ever heard of it; and 'sound scholar' is a term of praise applied to one another by learned men who have no reputation outside the University, and a rather queer one inside it. If you should write a book (you had better not), be sure that it is unreadable; otherwise you will be called 'brilliant' and forfeit all respect.

University printing presses exist, and are subsidized by the Government for the purpose of producing books which no one can read; and they are true to their high calling. Books are the sources of material for lectures They should be kept from the young; for to read books and remember what you read, well enough to reproduce it, is called cramming, and this is destructive of all true education. The best way to protect the young from books is, first, to make sure that they shall be so dry as to offer

no temptation; and, second, to store them in such a way that no one can find them without several years training. A lecturer is a sound scholar, who is chosen to teach on the ground that he was once able to learn. Eloquence is not permissible in a lecture; it is a privilege reserved by statute for the Public Orator.

VI. The Political Motive

You will begin, I suppose, by thinking that people who disagree with you and oppress you must be dishonest. Cynicism is the besetting and venial fault of declining youth, and disillusionment its last illusion. It is quite a mistake to suppose that real dishonesty is at all common. The number of rogues is about equal to the number of men who act honestly; and it is very small. The great majority would sooner behave honestly than not. The reason why they do not give way to this natural preference of humanity is that they are afraid that others will not; and the others do not because they are afraid that they will not. Thus it comes about that, while behaviour which looks dishonest is fairly common, sincere dishonesty is about as rare as the courage to evoke good faith in your neighbours by showing that you trust them.

No; the Political Motive in the academic breast is honest enough. It is *Fear* - genuine, perpetual, heartfelt timorousness. We shall see presently that all the Political Arguments are addressed to this passion. Have you ever noticed how people say 'I'm *afraid* I don't...' when they mean, 'I *think* I don't...'?

The proper objects of Fear, hereafter to be called *Bugbears*, are (in order of importance):

Giving yourself away;

Females;

What Dr - will say;

The Public Washing of Linen;

Socialism, otherwise Atheism;

198

The Great World; etc., etc., etc.

With the disclosure of this central mystery of academic politics, the theoretical part of our treatise is complete. The practical principles, to which we now turn, can nearly all be deduced from the nature of the political passion and of its objects.

The Practice of Politics may be divided under three heads: *Argument; The Conduct of Business; Squaring.*

VII. Argument

There is only one argument for doing something; the rest are arguments for doing nothing.

The argument for doing something is that it is the right thing to do. But then, of course, comes the difficulty of making sure that it is right. Females act by mere instinctive intuition; but men have the gift of reflection. As Hamlet, the typical man of action, says:

What is a man,
If his chief good and market of his time
Be but to sleep and feed? a beast, no more.
Sure, he that made us with such large discourse,
Looking before and after, gave us not
That capability and god-like reason
To fust in us unused

Now the academic person is to Hamlet as Hamlet is to a female; or, to use his own quaint phrase, a 'beast'; his discourse is many times larger, and he looks before and after many times as far. Even a little knowledge of ethical theory will suffice to convince you that all important questions are so complicated, and the results of any course of action are so difficult to foresee, that certainty, or even probability, is seldom, if ever, attainable. It follows at once that the only justifiable attitude of mind is suspense of judgment; and this attitude, besides being peculiarly congenial to the academic temperament, has the advantage of being comparatively easy to attain. There remains the duty of persuading others to be equally judicious, and to refrain from plunging into reckless courses which might lead them Heaven knows whither. At this point the arguments for doing nothing come in; for it is a mere theorist's paradox that doing nothing has just as many consequences as doing something. It is obvious that inaction can have no consequences at all.

Since the stone-axe fell into disuse at the close of the neolithic age, two other arguments of universal application have been added to the rhetorical armoury by the ingenuity of mankind. They are closely akin; and, like the stone-axe, they are addressed to the Political Motive. They are called the *Wedge* and the *Dangerous Precedent*. Though they are very familiar, the principles, or rules of inaction, involved in them are seldom stated in full. They are as follows.

The *Principle of the Wedge* is that you should not act justly now for fear of raising expectations that you may act still more justly in the future—expectations which you are afraid you will not have the courage to satisfy. A little reflection will make it evident that the Wedge argument implies the admission that the persons who use it cannot prove that the action is not just. If they could, that would be the sole and sufficient reason for not doing it, and this argument would be superfluous.

The *Principle of the Dangerous Precedent* is that you should not now do an admittedly right action for fear you, or your equally timid successors, should not have the courage to do right in some future case, which, *ex hypothesi*, is essentially different, but superficially resembles the present one. Every public action which is not customary, either is wrong, or, if it is right is a dangerous precedent. It follows that nothing should ever be done for the first time.

It will be seen that both the Political Arguments are addressed to the Bugbear of *Giving yourself away*. Other special arguments can be framed in view of the other Bugbears. It will often be sufficient to argue that a change is a change—an irrefutable truth. If this consideration is not decisive, it may be reinforced by the Fair Trial Argument—*'Give the present system a Fair Trial.'* This is especially useful in withstanding changes in the schedule of an examination. In this connection the exact meaning of the phrase is, 'I don't intend to alter my lectures if I can help it; and, if you pass this proposal, you will have to alter yours.' This paraphrase explains what might otherwise be obscure: namely, the reason why a Fair Trial ought only to be given to systems which already exist, not to proposed alternatives.

Another argument is that *'the Time is not Ripe'.* The Principle of Unripe Time is that people should not do at the present moment what they think right at that moment, because the moment at which they think it right has not yet arrived. But the unripeness of the time will, in some cases, be found to lie in the Bugbear, 'What Dr_ will say.' Time, by the way, is like the medlar; it has a trick; of going rotten before it is ripe.

VIII. The Conduct of Business

This naturally divides into two branches; (1) *Conservative Liberal Obstruction,* and (2) *Liberal Conservative Obstruction.*

The former is by much the more effective; and should always be preferred to mere unreasonable opposition, because it will bring you the reputation of being more advanced than any so-called reformer.

The following are the main types of argument suitable for the *Conservative Liberal.*

'The present measure would block the way for a far more sweeping reform.' The reform in question ought always to be one which was favoured by a few extremists in 1881, and which by this time is quite impracticable and not even desired by any one. This argument may safely be combined with the Wedge

argument: 'If we grant this, it will be impossible to stop short.' It is a singular fact that all measures are always opposed on both these grounds. The apparent discrepancy is happily reconciled when it comes to voting.

Another argument is that *'the machinery for effecting the proposed objects already exists.'* This should be urged in cases where the existing machinery has never worked, and is now so rusty that there is no chance of its being set in motion. When this is ascertained, it is safe to add that *'it is far better that all reform should come from within'*; and to throw in a reference to the *Principle of Washing Linen*. This principle is that it is better never to wash your linen if you cannot do it without anyone knowing that you are so cleanly.

The third accepted means of obstruction is the *Alternative Proposal*. This is a form of Red Herring. As soon as three or more alternatives are in the field, there is pretty sure to be a majority against any one of them, and nothing will be done.

The method of *Prevarication* is based upon a very characteristic trait of the academic mind, which comes out in the common remark, 'I was in favour of the proposal until I heard Mr_'s argument in support of it.' The principle is, that a few bad reasons for doing something neutralise all the good reasons for doing it. Since this is devoutly believed, it is often the best policy to argue weakly against the side you favour. If your personal enemies are present in force, throw in a little bear-baiting, and you are certain of success. You can vote in the minority, and no one will be the wiser.

Liberal Conservative Obstruction is less argumentative and leans to invective. It is particularly fond of the Last Ditch and the Wild Cat.

The *Last Ditch* is the Safe Side, considered as a place which you may safely threaten to die in. You are not likely to die there prematurely; for, to judge by the look of the inhabitants, the climate of the Safe Side conduces to longevity. If you did die, nobody would much mind; but the threat may frighten them for the moment.

'*Wild Cat*' is an epithet applicable to persons who bring forward a scheme unanimously agreed upon by experts after two years' exhaustive consideration of thirty-five or more alternative proposals. In its wider use it applies to all ideas which were not familiar in 1881.

There is an oracle of Merlin which says, 'When the wild cat is belled, the mice will vote *Placet.*'

The argument, '*that you remember exactly the same proposal being rejected in 1867,*' is a very strong one in itself; but its defect is that it appeals only to those who also remember the year 1867 with affectionate interest, and, moreover, are unaware that any change has occurred since then. There are such people, but they are lamentably few; and some even of them are no longer Young Men in a Hurry, and can be trusted to be on the Safe Side in any case. So this argument seldom carries its proper weight.

When other methods of obstruction fail, you should have recourse to *Wasting Time;* for, although it is recognised in academic circles that time in general is of no value, considerable importance is attached to teatime, and by deferring this, you may exasperate any body of men to the point of voting against anything. The simplest method is *Boring.* Talk slowly and indistinctly, at a little distance from the point. No academic person is ever voted into the chair until he has reached an age at which he has forgotten the meaning of the word 'irrelevant'; and you will be allowed to go on, until everyone in the room will vote with you sooner than hear your voice another minute. Then you should move for adjournment. Motions for adjournment, made less than fifteen minutes before teatime or at any subsequent moment, are always carried. While you are engaged in Boring it does not matter much what you talk about; but, if possible, you should discourse upon the proper way of doing something which you are notorious for doing badly yourself. Thus, if you are an inefficient lecturer, you should lay down the law on how to lecture; if you are a good business man, you should discuss the principles of finance and so on.

If you have applied yourself in youth to the cultivation of the *Private Business habit of mind* at the Union and other debating societies, questions of procedure will furnish you with many resources for wasting time. You will eagerly debate whether it is allowable or not to amend an amendment; or whether it is consonant with the eternal laws for a body of men, who have all changed their minds, to rescind a resolution which they have just carried. You will rise, like a fish, to points of order, and call your intimate friends 'honourable' to their faces. You will make six words do duty for one; address a harmless individual as if he were a roomful of abnormally stupid reporters; and fill up the time till you can think of something to say by talking, instead of by holding your tongue.

An appeal should be made, wherever it is possible, to *College Feeling*. This, like other species of patriotism, consists in a sincere belief that the institution to which you belong is better than an institution to which other people belong. The corresponding belief ought to be encouraged in others by frequent confession of this article of faith in their presence. In this way a healthy spirit of rivalry will be promoted. It is this feeling which makes the College System so valuable; and differentiates, more than anything else, a College from a boardinghouse; for in a boarding-house hatred is concentrated, not upon rival establishments, but upon the other members of the same establishment.

Should you have a taste for winter sports, you may amuse yourself with a little *Bear-baiting or Bullfighting*. Bulls are easier to draw than bears; you need only get to know the right red flag for a given bull, and for many of them almost any rag will serve the turn. Bears are more sulky and have to be prodded; on the other hand they don't go blind, like bulls; and when they have bitten your head off, they will often come round and be quite nice. Irishmen can be bulls, but not bears; Scotsmen can be bears, but not bulls; an Englishman may be either.

Another sport which wastes unlimited time is *Comma-hunting*. Once start a comma and the whole pack will be off, full cry, especially if they have had a literary training. (Adullamites affect to despise commas, and even their respect for syntax is often not above suspicion.) But comma-hunting is so exciting as to be a little dangerous. When attention is entirely concentrated on punctuation, there is some fear that the conduct of business may suffer, and a proposal get through without being properly obstructed on its demerits. It is therefore wise, when a kill has been made, to move at once for adjournment.

IX. Squaring

This most important branch of political activity is, of course, closely connected with *Jobs*. These fall into two classes, My Jobs and Your Jobs. My Jobs are public-spirited proposals, which happen (much to my regret) to involve the advancement of a personal friend, or (still more to my regret) of myself. Your Jobs are insidious intrigues for the advancement of yourself and your friends, speciously disguised as public-spirited proposals. The term Job is more commonly applied to the second class. When you and I have, each of us, a Job on hand, we shall proceed to go on the Square.

Squaring can be carried on at lunch; but it is better that we should meet casually. The proper course to pursue is to walk, between 2:00 and 4:00 p.m., up and down the King's Parade, and more particularly that part of it which lies between the Colleges of Pembroke and Caius. When we have succeeded in meeting accidentally, it is etiquette to talk about indifferent matters for ten minutes and then part. After walking five paces in the opposite direction you should call me back, and begin with the words, 'Oh, by the way, if you would happen...'. The nature of

Your Job must then be vaguely indicated, without mentioning names; and it should be treated by both parties as a matter of very small importance. You should hint that I am a very influential person, and that the whole thing is a secret between us. Then we shall part as before, and I shall call you back and introduce the subject of My Job, in the same formula. By observing this procedure we shall emphasise the fact that there is *no connection whatever* between my supporting your Job and your supporting mine. This absence of connection is the essential feature of Squaring.

Remember this: *the men who get things done are the men who walk up and down King's Parade, from 2 to 4 every day of their lives.* You can either join them, and become a powerful person; or you can join the great throng of those who spend all their time in preventing them from getting things done, and in the larger task of preventing one another from doing anything whatever. This is the Choice of Hercules, when Hercules takes to politics.

X. Farewell

O young academic politician, my heart is full of pity for you, because you will not believe a word that I have said. You will mistake sincerity for cynicism, and half the truth for exaggeration. You will think the other half of the truth, which I have not told, is the whole. You will take your own way, make yourself dreadfully disagreeable, tread on innumerable toes, butt your head against stone walls, neglect prejudice and fear, appeal to reason instead of appealing to bugbears. Your bread shall be bitterness, and your drink tears.

I have done what I could to warn you. When you become middle-aged—on your five-and-thirtieth birthday—glance through this book and judge between me and your present self.

If you decide that I was wrong, put the book in the fire, betake yourself to the King's Parade, and good-bye. I have done with you.

But if you find that I was right, remember that other world, within the microcosm, the silent, reasonable world, where the only action is thought, and thought is free from fear. If you go back to it now, keeping just enough bitterness to put a pleasant edge on your conversation, and just enough worldly wisdom to save other people's toes, you will find yourself in the best of all company — the company of clean, humorous intellect; and if you have a spark of imagination and try very hard to remember what it was like to be young, there is no reason why your brains should ever get woolly, or anyone should wish you out of the way. Farewell!

Explicit

# Recommended Resources

Buller, J. L. *The Essential Academic Dean.* San Francisco, CA: Jossy-Bass, 2007.
A balanced "view from the middle" as deans work between those to whom they report (The provost and the president) and those who report to them (department chairs, staff, students and faculty members).

Cornford, F. M. *Microcosmographia Academica.* Cambridge. Bowes and Bowes, 1908.
About the time my work as an administrator began, I discovered a book on the shelf of Professor Robert Haynes of York University in Toronto (a former colleague in biology at UC, Berkeley) titled *Microcosmographia Academica, Being A Guide for The Young Academic Politician* by Francis Macdonald Cornford, first published by Bowes and Bowes, Cambridge, in 1908. F. M. Cornford (1874–1943) was a distinguished classicist and Plato scholar at Cambridge University where he held the Laurence Professorship of Ancient Philosophy. He married Frances Darwin, the granddaughter of Charles Darwin, who shared his interest and abilities in poetry. His primary interest was in the relationship of philosophy to myth and in the evolution of the Greek mind. He

was also regarded as an unusually effective academic politician. We are fortunate that besides his translations of Plato, he left what may be an even more enduring work, *Microcosmographia Academica*, a remarkable little book that yields a perceptive and enduring insight into the faculty mind. It has been a delight to me ever since I discovered it.

Gunsalus, C. K. *The College Administrator's Survival guide.* **Cambridge, MA: Harvard University Press, 2006.**
A useful guide to the one-on-one challenges faced every day by a university administrator. Written with special attention to the legal boundary conditions which govern administration in today's universities.

Index

211

About Roderic B. Park

Dr. Park graduated from Harvard College in 1953, and subsequently earned his Ph.D. in plant biochemistry at the California Institute of Technology in 1958. He then spent thirty-four years at the University of California at Berkeley where he served as a department chair, Provost and Dean of the College of Letters and Science 1972–1980, and The Vice Chancellor (executive vice chancellor) 1980–1990. He became interim chancellor at CU Boulder for the period 1994–1997. During 2000–2001 he assisted the new UC Merced campus in hiring their first vice chancellors and deans, and led a detailed planning effort for implementation of the campus. During 2006–2007 he returned to the University of California at Merced as acting chancellor; he still serves as Senior Associate to the Chancellor. Over the past fifteen years he and his wife Catherine established the Rockpile Vineyard in Sonoma County, California, which is now recognized as an important producer of red wine grapes. He has served for five years as Chair of the Board of Visitors and Fellows for the Department of Viticulture and Enology at the University of California at Davis. In addition to having served on the Harvard Board of Overseers, Dr. Park also serves as a trustee on several other boards and foundations.